David Werner Amram

The Jewish Law of Divorce According to Bible and Talmud

With Some Reference to its Development in Post-Talmudic Times

David Werner Amram

The Jewish Law of Divorce According to Bible and Talmud
With Some Reference to its Development in Post-Talmudic Times

ISBN/EAN: 9783337138325

Printed in Europe, USA, Canada, Australia, Japan

Cover: Foto ©Suzi / pixelio.de

More available books at **www.hansebooks.com**

THE

Jewish Law of Divorce

ACCORDING TO

BIBLE AND TALMUD

WITH

SOME REFERENCE TO ITS DEVELOPMENT IN
POST-TALMUDIC TIMES

BY

DAVID WERNER AMRAM, M.A., LL.B., (Univ. of Penna.)

Member of the Philadelphia Bar

PHILADELPHIA
1896

DEDICATED

TO

MY FRIEND AND TEACHER

The REV. DR. MARCUS JASTROW

PREFACE.

IN the year 1888, a clergyman of the Protestant Episcopal Church was tried in the Ecclesiastical Court of the Diocese of Pennsylvania, upon the charges of immorality and breach of his ordination vow. His chief offense was his second marriage after he had been divorced from his first wife, because of her desertion, a ground of divorce not recognized by the Church. The most interesting question of law in the case arose out of the view which the Church took on the subject of Marriage and Divorce. The consideration of this question led me to inquire into the Jewish law on the subject as found in Bible and Talmud for the purpose of understanding the relation between two such apparently dissimilar texts as Deuteronomy xxiv, 1-4, and Matthew xix, 3-9.

Deeper interest in the subject led to further study and eventually to the preparation of the mass of accumulated material for publication.

May 16, 1896.

CONTENTS.

CHAPTER I.
INTRODUCTORY.

The Value of the Study of Biblical and Talmudic Laws—The Evolution of the Law—The Torah—The Chain of Oral Tradition—The Mishnah—The Disputes of the Pharisees and Sadducees—The Gemara—The Authority of the Talmud—The Codes of Maimonides, Asheri and Karo—The Law a Living Organism 9

CHAPTER II.
THE ANCIENT THEORY OF DIVORCE.

The Patriarch and his Family.—His Absolute Power—The Right of the Husband to Divorce his Wife at his Pleasure His Right pre-Mosaic—Restrictions laid upon him by the Deuteronomic Code—The Law of the False Accusation of Antenuptial Incontinence—The Law of the Ravisher.—The Protest of Malachi 22

CHAPTER III.
THE VIEWS OF THE TALMUDISTS AND OF JESUS.

The Discussion between the Schools of Hillel and Shammai—Philo—Josephus—The Dicta of Jesus—Ethical Views—Divorce by Mutual Consent—Divorce Sometimes Recommended 32

CHAPTER IV.

LAWS OF THE MISHNAH RESTRICTING THE HUSBAND'S RIGHT TO DIVORCE.

Modifying the Severity of the Biblical Laws of the False Accusation of Antenuptial Incontinence and of the Ravisher—The Insane Wife—The Captive—The Minor—The Formalities of Divorce Procedure—The Law of the Wife's Dowry—Denial of the Husband's Right to "Annul the Bill of Divorce"—When the Husband is *non compos mentis*— Deaf-Mute — The Culmination of these Restrictions in the Decree of Rabbi Gershom of Mayence................................. 41

CHAPTER V.

THE WIFE'S RIGHT TO SUE FOR DIVORCE.

The Germ of the Wife's Right Found in the Bible—Jurisdiction of the Courts to Compel the Husband to Grant the Bill of Divorce—The Question of Duress—The Acts of non-Jewish Courts—The Wife could Sue for Divorce, but could not Give a Bill of Divorce to her Husband—Influence of Roman Law during the last Days of the Jewish State 54

CHAPTER VI.

CAUSES ENTITLING THE WIFE TO A DIVORCE UNDER TALMUDIC LAW.

False Accusation of Antenuptial Incontinence — Refusal of Conjugal Rights—Impotence—Vow of Abstention—Priest's Wife—Physical Blemishes, etc.—Leprosy—Non-support—Restricting Wife's Lawful Freedom—Wife-beating—Desertion—Apostasy—Licentiousness—Divorce of Betrothed Wife .. 63

CONTENTS. 5

PAGE

CHAPTER VII.

RECONCILIATION AND REMARRIAGE.

Attempt to Reconcile the Couple a Duty of the Rabbis Under the Law—Rabbi was Legal and Spiritual Adviser—Absolving Husband from Vow to Divorce his Wife—Reconciliation after the Divorce has taken place—Remarriage of Divorced Couple—
—Prohibition of the Remarriage of the Divorced Couple after the Wife had been Married to Another—The Deuteronomic Law—Views of Philo and Jesus—Mohammedan Law—The Issue of such Unlawful Marriage is nevertheless Legitimate—Other Persons whom the Divorced Wife may not Marry 78

CHAPTER VIII.

JUDICIAL SEPARATIONS UNDER THE QUASI-CRIMINAL JURISDICTION OF THE RABBIS.

Incest—Marriage of Hebrew and Heathen—The Great Reform of Ezra — Mamzer— Nethin — Adulteress and Paramour—The Ordeal of the Bitter Waters—Lepers—Forbidden Marriages of the Priests—Remarriage of the Divorced Couple after the Wife had been Married to Another—Yebama—Childless Marriages 89

CHAPTER IX.

THE LEGAL AND SOCIAL STATUS OF THE DIVORCED WOMAN.

Divorced Woman is *Sui Juris*—Cannot Marry a Kohen (Priest)—Under the Old Law no Odium Attached to the Divorced Woman—Change Under Later Law

—Divorced Woman Liable for her Torts—Bound by her Vows—She may Give Herself in Marriage to Anyone—If Suspected of Adultery she Cannot Marry her Paramour—Nor the Messenger Bringing her Bill of Divorce—Nor the Rabbi who Refuses to Absolve her Vows—She must not Marry within Three Months after her Divorce   101

CHAPTER X.

THE PROPERTY RIGHTS OF THE DIVORCED WOMAN AND THE CUSTODY AND MAINTENANCE OF HER CHILDREN.

The Kethubah—The Biblical Dowry—The Ordinance of Shimeon ben Shetaḥ—The Lien of the Kethubah—The Wife could not Waive her Rights under the Kethubah—Dowry at Mohammedan Law—The Amount of the Kethubah—Increase of the Kethubah—Payment of the Kethubah - Wife's Separate Estate — Earnings, etc., of Divorced Wife — Prescriptive Rights against her Former Husband—Cases in which the Divorced Wife lost her Kethubah by Reason of her Misconduct—Custody of Children of Divorced Woman —Nurslings—Roman Law as to Custody—Rabbinical Decisions - Support of Children at Roman Law and Jewish Law. . .   111

CHAPTER XI.

THE BILL OF DIVORCE (GET).

Antiquity of the Bill of Divorce — Supposed by Rabbinical Writers to have been known to Abraham —Peculiar to the Jews —Arabian Form of Divorce — Form of Divorce among Greeks and Romans— Bills of Divorce prepared in the non-Jewish Courts   132

CONTENTS. 7

CHAPTER XII.

PREPARING THE BILL OF DIVORCE (GET).

Divorce Procedure, at first Simple, Became Complex—Husband Must Give the Order to Prepare the Get with the Intention of Divorcing His Wife—What is Deemed a Sufficient Order to the Scribe and Witnesses—Exceptions in Favor of Persons in Situation of Danger, etc.—Uses of the Bill of Divorce—Divorce by a Mute Husband—Writing the Get—The Scribe—Fees of the Scribe—The Writing Materials 142

CHAPTER XIII.

THE FORM OF THE BILL OF DIVORCE (GET) AND THE GET "ON CONDITION."

Maimonides' Form — Blank Forms—The Folded Get—The Essentials of a Get—Date—*Dies juridici*—Names — Words of Separation — Clauses in Restraint of Marriage —The Get "On Condition"—Origin of the Right of the Husband to Annex Conditions to his Bill of Divorce—Wife Could Accept or Reject—Condition Must be Strictly Complied With—On Condition of the Husband's Death—On Condition of his Failure to Return 156

CHAPTER XIV.

ATTESTATION AND DELIVERY OF THE BILL OF DIVORCE (GET).

The Get was Attested by Two Witnesses—Who were Personally Acquainted with the Husband and Wife—The Delivery of the Get was Essential to Complete the Divorce—Method of Delivery—Delivery to Minor Wife—Delivery by Messenger—Presumption that the Husband is Alive at the Time the Messenger delivers the Get—Who may be Messenger — The Messengers of the Husband — The Messengers of the Wife—Sub-Messengers   171

CHAPTER XV.

WHEN THE GET IS NULL AND VOID, OR LOST.

The Husband's Right to Annul the Get Denied by Rabban Gamaliel—Attempts by Common Barrators to Cast Doubt on Divorce Proceeding—Ban of Excommunication—Proof of Divorce when Get is Lost —Uncorroborated Statement of the Divorced Wife   186

CHAPTER XVI.

SEDER HA-GET.

Rules of Procedure in Divorce, as reported by Rabbi Joseph Karo in the Shulḥan Arukh, Treatise Eben Haüzer, Section 154, with occasional notes by Rabbi Moses Isserles   192
List of Principal Works Consulted   205
Glossary   209
Index   215

CHAPTER I.

INTRODUCTORY.

The Value of the Study of Biblical and Talmudic Laws—The Evolution of the Law—The Torah—The Chain of Oral Tradition—The Mishnah—The Disputes of the Pharisees and Sadducees—The Gemara—The Authority of the Talmud—The Codes of Maimonides, Asheri and Karo—The Law a Living Organism.

SIR HENRY SUMNER MAINE, in his epoch-making "Ancient Law," calls attention, in several passages, to the almost universal neglect of the laws of the ancient Hebrews by students of comparative jurisprudence and the philosophy of the law. He shows how the study of the Biblical records would have corrected the errors of the philosophers of France during the latter part of the eighteenth century. In that period of intellectual travail, when society was drifting from its ancient moorings and the philosophers were trying to devise a system of law in harmony with the new social conditions, "there was but one body of primitive records which was worth studying—the early history of the Jews. But resort to this was prevented by the prejudices of the time. One of the few characteristics which the school of Rousseau had in common with the school of Voltaire was an utter disdain of all religious antiquities; and, more than all, of those of the Hebrew race. It is well known that it was a point of honour with the reasoners of that day to assume, not merely that the institutions called after Moses were not divinely dictated, nor even that they were codified at a later date than that attributed to them, but that they and the entire Pentateuch were a gratuitous forgery, executed after the return from the Captivity. Debarred, therefore, from one chief security against speculative delusion, the philosophers of France, in their eagerness to escape from what they deemed a superstition of the priests, flung themselves headlong into a superstition of the lawyers" (*i. e.*, The Theory of the Law of Nature).[1]

While it is true that the character of the prejudice against the use of the Hebrew records has changed during the last hundred years, there still remains, as Maine says in another passage, "a disposition to undervalue these accounts, or rather to decline generalizing from them, as forming part of the traditions of a Semitic people."[2]

If this is true of the Hebrew Scriptures, which have become the heritage of all civilized men, it is all the more true of the body of Jewish law preserved in the Talmud and the Rabbinical writings. This system of law, the growth of ages, has not yet received that share of unprejudiced attention which it deserves.

The student of comparative jurisprudence can

---

[1] Maine's "Ancient Law," p. 86, *et seq*.
[2] Idem, p. 118.

no longer neglect the remarkable legal system of the Hebrews, which had its rise before the beginnings of the Roman law, and which still regulates the life and conduct of several millions of men in our own day.

The peculiar laws of marriage and divorce, for instance, as well as other branches of the jurisprudence of the Hebrews, the origin of which is buried in the mists of antiquity, have come down to our time in an unbroken chain of judicial decisions and expositions. In the length of time through which it extends and in the numerous modifications which it has undergone, the system of jurisprudence peculiar to the Jews stands absolutely unique.

For the student of the Jewish law, the Bible is the fountain-head of information, the most ancient record to which he can turn. Although it is very likely that the nomadic tribes of the Hebrews were in the course of their wanderings affected by the laws and customs of many different peoples, yet the present state of our knowledge of the laws and the institutions of those ancient peoples precludes an attempt to trace their influence on the laws and customs of the Hebrews. Beginning with the Bible and following the law downward through the centuries, it is seen expanding and growing and reaching out to cover the plexus of events and conditions of human life, constantly changing under the influence of time and clime and circumstance. To the Rabbis, the Doctors of the Law, it was a growing science, a living organism. In their discussions in the Schools of the Law, as well as in the decisions of the cases that came before them, they did not exhibit a mere blind adherence to ancient precept. Although prompted by their religious convictions to be conservative, they cautiously, often unconsciously, advanced. The growth of law is evolutionary. The strict letter of the law soon becomes an anachronism; for every system of law, however rigid, must yield to the subtle but irresistible influence of the changing conditions of human life.

The Mosaic law, the foundation of the legal system of the Hebrews, cannot be understood unless it is read by the light of its commentary, the Talmud. The law of divorce, for example, cannot be said to exist in the Biblical code at all, there being but a few scattered and incidental references to it found in the Book of Deuteronomy. These few references grew into volumes of law in the Talmud and Rabbinical writings; the simple norms of a race of agriculturists and herdsmen developed into the complex system of law demanded by the highly developed civilization of a nation.

The Bible itself cannot be properly considered the fountain-head from which the law takes its origin, for when the Lawgiver compiled this code, he was even then summing up, in a concise form, many of the customs and laws that had existed in former times among the Hebrews.

Many of these ancient customs and laws may be traced in the Biblical records, and others have been preserved in nooks and corners of the Talmud.

The traditions of the Patriarchs, the records of the Judges and Kings, as well as the inspired writings of the Prophets, contain many allusions to ancient law. Biblical legislation has given body and substance to much of the old traditional folk-law, and the whole Bible is a storehouse of reference to which the Rabbis turned for rules and principles to govern their discussions and decisions. Although the Rabbis were firm believers in the divine inspiration of the Bible, they were by no means slaves to its letter; while believing it to be the word of God, they applied sound reason and common sense to its interpretation, and recognized these as the only legitimate means to resolve its meaning in doubtful cases.

The decisions of the Rabbis are preserved in the Mishnah, a code of law supplementary to the Bible. The Mishnah is the Oral Law as distinguished from the Bible, the Written Law, and is not properly to be considered as following the Bible, but as contemporaneous with it. We know when the code of the Mishnah was compiled, but its origins are lost in antiquity. The Mishnah itself bears testimony to its ancient traditional origin. One of its divisions, the so-called "Sayings of the Fathers," (Pirqé Aboth) opens with the following statement of the chain of tradition: "Moses received the Law at Sinai, and he transmitted it to Joshua, and Joshua to the Elders, and the Elders to the Prophets, and the Prophets handed it down to the Men of the Great Synagogue,"[1] and

---

[1] Aboth i, 1.

the last of the members of the Great Synagogue was Simon the Just, who lived at the beginning of the third century B. C. E. This law, thus transmitted, was divided into two parts, the written and the oral law, or, as we might call it, statutory and case law. The written law was the Pentateuch (Torah) and it was transmitted from generation to generation without change or modification; the oral law, according to tradition, also began with Moses, and was a contemporaneous commentary on the Torah.

In the introduction to his monumental code of the Jewish Law, (1180 C. E.) Maimonides gives the following account of the tradition of the law: "All the laws given to Moses at Sinai were given together with their commentary, for it is written, And I will give thee tables of stone and a law (Torah) and commandments (Miçvoth).[1] The Torah is the written law and the Miçvoth are the commentaries; and he commanded us to perform the law according to its commentary, and this commentary is called the Oral Law. Moses, our teacher, himself wrote the entire Torah, and he gave a copy thereof to each tribe, and one copy was laid in the Ark, as a witness; as it is written, Take this Book of the Law and put it in the side of the Ark of the Covenant of the Lord your God, that it may be there as a witness against thee.[2] And the commandments (Miçvoth), which were the commentary on the Law, he did not write down,

[1] Exodus xxiv, 12.
[2] Deuteronomy xxxi, 26.

but he commanded them unto the Elders and unto Joshua and the rest of Israel; as it is written, Whatever thing I command you, observe to do it.[1] On this account it is called the Oral Law. Although the oral law was not written down, Moses, our teacher, taught the whole of it in his Court of Justice to the Seventy Elders; . . . and to Joshua, who was the pupil of Moses, our teacher, he transmitted the oral law and instructed him in it; and many Elders received it from Joshua and his Court of Law, and Eli received it from the Elders and from Phineas, and Samuel received it from Eli and his Court of Law, and David received it from Samuel and his Court of Law." And through him the law was transmitted to the Prophets and expounded in their Courts of Law, and from them Ezra received it; and the judges of the Court of Ezra were called the Men of the Great Synagogue, and the last of them was Simon the Just.[2]

According to this account, which contains in it the actual fact, though somewhat fancifully embellished by tradition, the oral law was expounded in the court of justice, presided over by Moses, and after him by successive generations of judges, contemporaneous with and following the Biblical period. From the time of Simon the Just (about 300 B. C. E.) to the time of Rabbi Yehudah the Nasi (about 200 C. E.), the compiler of the Mishnah, there was an unbroken sequence of Judges and Rabbis who expounded and interpreted the law and the account of whose

[1] Deuteronomy xii, 32.
[2] Introduction to Maimonides' Mishné Torah.

personality and judicial decisions rests upon no mere vague tradition, but is well established and authenticated. These were the Tannaïm (Learners).

The Mishnah or oral law, as expounded by the Tannaïm, was generally accepted by the people, but met with strong opposition from the ruling classes, the princes and the priests, who formed the backbone of the class known in history as the Sadducees, so called to distinguish them from the people, the Pharisees. The Pharisaic judges expounded the law rationally and sought to harmonize it with the new conditions of life that arose from time to time; the Sadducees, on the other hand, were strict conservatives, who would have none of the interpretation of the law by the Rabbis, and who held to the very letter of the Bible. Their views were exceedingly narrow, and they departed not from the ways of their fathers. They deemed it a desecration, for example, to insert the name of a heathen sovereign, in dating a Bill of Divorce, because, forsooth, the Bill of Divorce contained the name of Moses, whose memory was thereby insulted. The Pharisees very pertinently pointed out to them that the Bible itself places the name of the heathen Pharaoh on the same page with that of God.[1] In another case the Sadducees argued, in conformity with the letter of the Biblical law, that a man is liable in damages for the injury done by his slave. For they said, as we are liable for the damage caused by our animals, respecting which we have no religious duties, we must cer-

[1] Mishnah Yadayim iv, 8.

tainly be liable for the damage done by our slave, for whose religious and moral welfare we are obliged to care. But the Pharisees answered this specious argument by showing that the rules which may be applied to the case of the ox and the ass, which are not possessed of reason, are not applicable to the case of the slave, who is a rational being; for if the master were held liable for the acts of his slave, the latter might, in revenge for some wrong done to him by the master, set fire to the growing corn of another person, to compel his master to pay for it.[1]

Thus, although not accepted by the Sadducees, the oral law grew and developed, and found favor among the people because of its reasonableness.

The *terminus ad quem* of the Mishnah is the compilation or Code of Rabbi Yehudah the Nasi, framed about 200 C. E. Rabbi Yehudah codified the ancient Mosaic laws and their numerous judicial interpretations, and these (the Mishnah) became in their turn *The Law*, the basis of a new commentary, the Gemara.[2]

The Rabbinical authorities of the period of the Gemara are known as the Amoraïm, their work being characterized by a close study and discussion of the Mishnah, and their arguments being given at length in the Talmud. During the time of the

[1] Mishnah Yadayim iv, 7.
[2] There were two Gemaras, the Gemara of Jerusalem, or, more properly, of Palestine, and the Gemara of Babylon. These contain the decisions and discussions that arose after the compilation of the Mishnah. The Mishnah and Gemara together are known as the Talmud.

Amoraïm, the centre of Jewish life and learning was shifted from Palestine to Babylonia. The schools and colleges of Palestine were gradually deserted, and Babylonia became the home of the law. In Sura, Nahardea, Pumbaditha and Mahuza flourishing schools arose, and it was here especially that that enormous body of precept and argument known as the Babylonian Talmud was framed. This contains not only the decisions of practical questions, of cases brought before the courts, but also the theoretical discussions of legal questions in the Schools of Law.[1]

The Talmud became the authoritative exposition of the law for all Israel scattered in the four corners of the world. The wide dispersion led to certain differences in minor points of practice, the interpretation of the law being affected by the individual views of Rabbis and the local peculiarities and characteristics of the people; but in all important matters the law was uniformly determined by the Talmud.

In the year 1180 C. E., Maimonides completed his Code of the Law. This contains the entire law from the days of Moses ben Amram to the days of Moses ben Maimon, and was intended, as Maimonides states in his preface, to settle all differences and to supersede all other Talmudical and Rabbinical

---

[1] The Talmud is not merely a law book, but an "Encyclopedia of Jewish life." The classical essay of Emanuel Deutsch on "The Talmud," published among his "Literary Remains" and recently republished by the Jewish Publication Society, at Philadelphia, will give the reader some adequate idea of the meaning of that term.

works. The entire law is therein set forth without discussion in simple and sententious phraseology. It is carefully and scientifically divided and subdivided, so that any law may readily be found in it, and is a monument to the greatness and learning of its author.

The code of Maimonides, however, became the subject of further discussion and comment, and the volume of Rabbinical law grew apace. Several codes were compiled in various parts of the world, the most important and comprehensive being the code of Jacob ben Asher, of Toledo (1340), called Turim, which was based especially on the code of Maimonides,[1] and the code of Joseph Karo of Adrianople, based upon the Turim and completed by its author after thirty-two years of labor, in the year 1554. This is the famous Shulḥan Arukh from which the laws and the religion of the Jews received the form which they have preserved up to the present time.[2]

The Jewish law is embodied in this series of Codes, from the Bible to the Shulḥan Arukh. They all were attempts at systematizing the enormous volume of law which was always growing and changing under the decisions of the courts.

The development of the law cannot be checked, for new conditions arise which the wisest lawgiver cannot foresee, and these must have their law. The laws of Moses were, in the course of centu-

---

[1] Graetz's "History of the Jews," American Edition, Vol. IV, pp. 88, etc.
[2] Graetz's "History of the Jews," Vol. IV, p. 612, etc.

ries, to a large extent superseded by the laws of the Mishnah, these in turn were gradually modified and changed throughout the period of the Gemara. The impossibility of laying down immutable laws was manifest to the Rabbis. "If the law had been completely given without permission to modify it," said Rabbi Yannai (about 220 C. E.), a leading authority in his time, "men could not exist, for it is only in consequence of discussion of the learned that the law is moulded to meet the conditions of life. Moses asked God to teach him the Halakhah (law, rule of action), and God told him to find it in the voice of the majority."[1]

The new laws and the modification of old laws were necessary on account of the changing conditions of life. It was by virtue of their very necessity that they were considered no less sacred than the laws of the Bible. "The ordinances of the Rabbis have an authority equal to the laws of the Torah,"[2] of which they were a necessary supplement and continuation.

It will be seen from what has gone before, that the study of the laws of the Bible without the use of the Talmud is the study of the law without the commentary; it is an attempt to understand the character of a nation by reading its statute book, and disregarding the judicial interpretation and application of its laws to the daily life of the people. The results of such study are necessarily meagre.

The laws of the Bible do not, as so many sup-

[1] Talmud Yerushalmi Sanhedrin sub Mishnah iv, 2 (22 a).
[2] Talmud Babli Pessaḥim 30 b.

pose, stand alone and unique in history, but they have a long line of legal ancestors and descendants, and are merely one link in the chain which extended from the ancient law of the patriarchal family to the latest Rabbinical interpretation of a section of the Shulḥan Arukh.

CHAPTER II.

THE ANCIENT THEORY OF DIVORCE.

The Patriarch and his Family—His Absolute Power—The Right of the Husband to Divorce his Wife at his Pleasure—His Right pre-Mosaic—Restrictions Laid upon him by the Deuteronomic Code—The Law of the False Accusation of Antenuptial Incontinence—The Law of the Ravisher—The Protest of Malachi.

THE origins of law are to be found in the constitution of the patriarchal family, and the fundamental principle of its government was the absolute authority of the oldest male ascendant, who was the lawgiver and the judge, and whose rule over his wives, children and slaves was supreme.[1] This was the power of the husband and father by virtue of his rank in the family, and this, in the theory of the law, remained his right throughout the subsequent history of the Jewish people, although in the course of time it was greatly modified and curtailed.

Among the early traditions of the Hebrews, there are many instances illustrating the absolute power and authority of the Patriarch.

[1] Maine's "Ancient Law" passim. It is true that there was a legal system and a social life anterior to the patriarchal, and differing from it; but it has left no traces in the Jewish divorce law.

Jephthah, Judge of Israel, sacrificed his daughter in fulfilment of a rash vow made by him when he set out in the war against the Ammonites.[1] Abraham likewise was prepared to sacrifice his son Isaac as an offering to his God.[2] King Saul gave away his daughter, Mikhal, to another man, although she had been previously married to David;[3] a right similar to that which the Roman father had over his married daughter, who had not yet passed out of his *manus*.[4]

Among the traditions of the Patriarch Abraham is found another illustration of this right, and one more pertinent to our subject. Sarah, after the birth of her son Isaac, was displeased with Hagar and her son Ishmael, and she prevailed upon Abraham to "cast out this bondwoman and her son." Very much against his inclination, Abraham did as Sarah requested, and the account of this casting out or divorce of Hagar is given with naïve simplicity. "And Abraham arose early in the morning and took bread and a bottle of water and gave it unto Hagar, putting it on her shoulder, and the child, and sent her away."[5] Hagar, although she had apparently attained the dignity of wifehood,[6] was sent away without much formality.

[1] Judges xi, 30, 40.
[2] Genesis xxii, 1-12.
[3] 1 Samuel xxv, 44; 2 Samuel iii, 14.
[4] Code of Justinian, Book v, Tit. 17, Const. 5. The Philistines (Judges xiv, 20-xv, 2) and the Chinese (Letourneau, "Evolution of Marriage and the Family," p. 184) anciently had the same right.
[5] Genesis xxi, 9-14.
[6] Genesis xvi, 3.

The further back that we trace the history of institutions, and especially of domestic relations, the greater we find this power of the father and husband; not only affecting the legal status of the wife, but controlling her actions, her property and her person. At the very beginning, or, at least, as far back as the history of this institution can be traced, the husband's right to divorce was absolutely untrammelled, and it was only with the gradual breaking up of the patriarchal system, and the substitution of an individualistic for a socialistic state, that the woman acquired, at first merely negative rights, such as protection against her husband's acts, and, finally, positive rights, under which she could proceed against him.

This ancient right of the husband, to divorce his wife at his pleasure, is the central thought in the entire system of Jewish divorce law; and the Rabbis did not, nor could they, set it aside, although, as will be shown hereafter, they gradually tempered its severity by numerous restrictive measures. Rabbinical ethics in this as in other cases outstripped the law, which lagged centuries behind, and it was not until the eleventh century of the common era that, by the decree of Rabbi Gershom, of Mayence, the absolute right of the husband to divorce his wife at will was *formally* abolished, although it had already been *practically* non-existent in Talmudic times.

The view that has been above set forth, that the theory of the ancient Jewish common law considered divorce a private right of the husband, established by immemorial custom, is not generally accepted, and certain ethical dicta of the Old and New Testament are cited against it. It is commonly supposed that Moses permitted divorce because of his people's hardness of heart; and that from the beginning it was not so; that the pre-Mosaic law forbade divorce and did not attempt to put asunder what God hath joined together. In support of this view the words of Genesis are quoted. "And the man (Adam) said, This time it is bone of my bones and flesh of my flesh; this shall be called Woman (Ishah) because out of Man (Ish) was this one taken; therefore doth a man leave his father and his mother and cleave unto his wife and they become one flesh."[1] But it is an error to suppose that these high ethical conceptions of the marriage relation were carried out in actual practice. Divorce was and is a necessary evil, so considered in all civilized society. Theoretically, men have always agreed that the lofty sentiments expressed both in the Old and the New Testament constituted the ideals that should govern a perfect marriage. But the practice of men, as well in the dim antiquity of the pre-Mosaic age as in the eighteen hundred years since the establishment of Christianity, has recognized the necessity of divorce, while regretting its nonconformity with the ideals that should govern the marriage relation. And, indeed, it will be observed on closer inspection that the sayings both of Hebrew and Christian moralists in condemnation

[1] Genesis ii, 23-24.

of divorce are directed not against the exercise of this right, but against its abuse. Jesus himself felt obliged to recognize the validity of divorce, although he confined it to cases of the wife's fornication.[1] The Jewish law recognized the validity of divorce in all cases, and sought to prevent its abuse by moral injunction and judicial regulation. The Old Testament, written at a time when the domestic law of the patriarchal family was in full vigor, accepted divorce as a matter of fact, as an institution that had existed since time immemorial. The modern law of all civilized states has recognized divorce as a necessity; and it is a notorious fact that those states which have unduly restricted the liberty of divorce have on record a much greater proportion of sexual crime and immorality than those that have adopted liberal divorce laws.

The earliest restrictions upon the patriarchal right of the husband to divorce his wife at will are found in the Deuteronomic Code.[2] The curtail-

---

[1] Matthew xix, 9.

[2] The original Deuteronomic Code has, since the publication of the researches of De Wette in 1805, been almost universally accepted by Biblical scholars to be the same code of law referred to as the "Book of the Covenant" in the Second Book of Kings. It is there recorded that in the eighteenth year of King Josiah (about 621 B. C. E.), a Book of the Law was found in the Temple by the High Priest, who gave it to Shaphan, the king's scribe. "And Shaphan, the scribe, told the king, saying, A book hath Hilkiah, the Priest, given me; and Shaphan read it before the king." The king was powerfully affected on hearing the words of the Book, and, having summoned his people to the Temple Mount, "he read in their ears all the words of the Book of the Cove-

ment of the husband's right naturally proceeded by slow degrees, and the old records in Deuteronomy show but two cases in which it was restricted, and in these cases only for the weightiest moral reasons. Many analogies are to be found in modern times, in cases where the statutory law has gradually eaten out the heart of some old common law doctrine. A familiar instance is the law relating to married women's property rights. It is only towards the end of the nineteenth century that the liberalizing modern spirit has, by a series of legislative acts, freed the married woman from the yoke of the ancient common law.

Legislative interference with ancient customary right was at all times objectionable to the mass of the people. Moses called his people "stiffnecked."[1] This simply means that they were conservative and therefore ill-disposed to accept the innovations suggested by him, even though they had divine sanction. They preferred their ancient idolatry to his monotheism; their old household law to his new system, and no doubt their ancient privilege of sending away their wives to his restric-

nant, which was found in the House of the Lord" (2 Kings, chaps. 22 and 23 passim). This Book of the Covenant was the basis of the great religious and legal reforms of King Josiah, which mark a turning point in the history of Israel.—Graetz's "History of the Jews" (American Edition, Philadelphia, 1891), Vol. I, pp. 292-296.

For discussion of this question and collation of authorities see article "Pentateuch" in Encyclopædia Britannica, Ninth Edition; and also Cornill's "Einleitung in das Alte Testament," Edition 1892, p. 31, *et seq.*

[1] Deuteronomy ix, 6.

tive measures, though the latter were neither many nor unreasonable.

Turning now to Deuteronomy we find in it but two laws restricting the husband's right of divorce.

In the first of these the husband is punished for falsely accusing his wife of antenuptial incontinence, by being deprived of his right to divorce her and being compelled to keep her as his wife forever. "If a man take a wife and go near unto her and hate her, and he lay an accusation against her and spread abroad an evil name upon her and say, this woman I took and when I came near to her I found no tokens of virginity in her; then shall the father of the damsel and her mother take and bring forth the tokens of the damsel's virginity[1] unto the elders of the city to the gate. And the father of the damsel shall say unto the elders, 'My daughter I gave unto this man for a wife, but he hates her, and behold he has laid an accusation, saying, I have found no tokens of virginity in thy daughter, and yet these are the tokens of my daughter's virginity;' and they shall spread the garment before the elders of the city. And the elders of the city shall take that man and chastise him and they shall amerce him in a hundred (shekels) of silver and give them unto the father of the damsel, because he has spread abroad an evil name upon a virgin of Israel; and *she shall be*

[1] Among the country folk in Russia this custom still prevails.—Maxime Kovalevsky, " Modern Customs and Ancient Laws of Russia " (London, 1891), p. 43, *et seq*.

his wife; he shall not be at liberty to put her away all his days."[1]

Further on, in the same chapter, is found the second law, by which a similar punishment is prescribed for the ravisher:—

"If a man find a damsel that is a virgin, who is not betrothed, and lay fast hold on her, and lie with her, and they be found; then shall the man who lay with her, give unto the father of the damsel fifty (shekels) of silver and *she shall be his wife; because he has humbled her, he shall not be at liberty to put her away all his days.*"[2]

Before the enactment of these laws the husband was under no restriction whatever, and could divorce his wife whenever it pleased him to do so. By these laws his liberty received its first check. The deprivation of the right to divorce was one of the penalties inflicted upon him because of an infamous slander, or of rape. To compel a man to keep and support a woman all her life, in a society where all enjoyed the utmost freedom in sending away their wives, must have been a very severe punishment.

Divorce is incidentally mentioned in another law in Deuteronomy. "If a man has taken a wife and

[1] Deuteronomy xxii, 13-19.
[2] Ibid. 28-29. In Exodus xxii, 16-17, a similar enactment provides that the man who seduces a girl "shall endow her to be his wife," but that if her father refuses to give her unto him, "he shall pay money according to the dowry of virgins." The subject of the dowry of brides (Kethubah) will be taken up in another chapter. It is closely interwoven with the divorce laws of the Talmud.

married her, and it come to pass that she finds no favor in his eyes, because he has found something unseemly in her, and he writes her a bill of divorce and gives it into her hand and sends her out of his house; and she departs from his house and goes and becomes another man's (wife); and the latter husband hates her and writes her a bill of divorce and gives it into her hand and sends her away out of his house, or if the latter husband who took her as his wife should die: then shall not her former husband who has sent her away, be at liberty to take her again to be his wife, after she has been defiled." [1]

The purpose of this law was to prevent the remarriage of a divorced woman to her first husband after she had been "defiled" by a second marriage.

The spirit of Biblical ethics is opposed to all forms of violence and injustice, and the dismissal of the wife without cause was no doubt felt to be wrong. But outraged morality did not find voice in the Bible until Malachi opened his lips to denounce what was the great wrong of his day.

Upon the return of the Israelites from captivity in Babylon (537 B. C. E.), some of them divorced their Jewish wives and united themselves in marriage with the heathen women among whom they had taken up their abode in Palestine. Against this wanton dismissal of their wives the prophet Malachi raised his voice in no uncertain tone. The law was powerless to prevent this divorcing, but

[1] Deuteronomy xxiv, 1-4.

morality could not countenance it. "Because the Eternal has been witness between thee and the wife of thy youth against whom thou hast dealt treacherously, yet she is thy companion and the wife of thy covenant. . . . Let none deal treacherously against the wife of his youth. For I hate him that puts away his wife, said the Eternal God of Israel."[1]

The voice of Malachi re-echoed in many dicta of the Talmudic moralists, who condemned the practice of hasty and groundless divorce which the law allowed.

[1] Malachi ii, 14-16.

CHAPTER III.

THE VIEWS OF THE TALMUDISTS AND OF JESUS.

The Discussion between the Schools of Hillel and Shammai
—Philo—Josephus—The Dicta of Jesus—Ethical Views
—Divorce by Mutual Consent—Divorce Sometimes
Recommended.

THE review of this question thus far shows the right to divorce to have been a private right of the husband, the natural outgrowth of the patriarchal system, and to be exercised by him at his pleasure, except in the two cases in which the Deuteronomic code has restricted it:—the case of the ravisher and of the one who falsely accuses his wife of antenuptial incontinence.[1] Although the theory of the law remained the same throughout the period of the Mishnah, it did not pass unchallenged, and was, in practice, modified in various ways. The question had evidently been the subject of conflicting judicial interpretation during the first century before the Christian era, for the schools of Hillel and Shammai, the two great doctors of the law who flourished at that time, held radically different views on the subject.

The school of Shammai interpreted nearly all the Biblical laws strictly and rigorously. They

[1] Deuteronomy xxii, 13-19; 28-29.

were, to use a term applied to certain interpreters of the Constitution of the United States, Strict Constructionists; they held that a man cannot divorce his wife unless he has found her guilty of sexual immorality.¹ This doctrine, so completely at variance with the customary right of the husband, was based upon a peculiar interpretation of the words "something unseemly" in the Deuteronomic law above quoted.² They held that these words (Hebrew, *Ervath Dabar;* literally, "the nakedness of the matter"), signified sexual immorality; and that the old law recognized this as the only legitimate cause for divorce.

The School of Hillel, on the other hand, were generally more liberal in their interpretation of the Biblical laws, and were the Broad Constructionists of the Bible. They held that the husband need not assign any reason whatever for his divorce, and that he may, for instance, if he please, divorce his wife for spoiling his food.³ They also rested their opinion on the authority of the Deuteronomic text, and interpreted the words "something unseemly" to mean anything offensive to the husband.

One hundred years later the question was still a subject of debate, although the ancient theory supported by the School of Hillel seems to have been generally accepted. Rabbi Aqiba (died about 135 C. E.), whose opinion was of commanding authority, held with the School of Hillel that a

¹ Mishnah Gittin ix, 10; Talmud Yerushalmi Sotah I,i (16 b).
² Deuteronomy xxiv, 1-4.
³ Mishnah Gittin ix, 10.

man need assign no reason for divorcing his wife, and may, for example, divorce her if he find another woman more beautiful than she, for it is written, "if she find no favor in his eyes."[1] The same opinion was held by Philo of Alexandria (10 B. C. E. to 60 C. E.), one of the most distinguished philosophers and jurists of his time. In his treatise "Of Special Laws," in commenting on the law of Deuteronomy, he says:[2] "If a woman, having been divorced from her husband, *under any pretence whatever*, and having married another, has again become a widow, whether her second husband is alive or dead, still she must not return to her former husband." In theory, Philo held, the wife could be divorced by the husband at his will, and his right to divorce her did not depend upon the Deuteronomic Law, but was an ancient customary right.

Flavius Josephus (38–95 C. E.), in his "Antiquities of the Jews," shares the opinion of the School of Hillel, that a man may divorce his wife for any reason whatever. "He who desires to be divorced from his wife for any cause whatsoever, and many such causes happen among men, let him in writing give assurance that he no longer wishes to live with her as his wife."[3]

[1] Mishnah Gittin ix, 10.
[2] Philo Judæus, "Of Special Laws Relating to Adultery, etc.," Chap. 5. English Edition of Yonge, in Bohn's Library, Vol. III, pp. 310, 311.
[3] Josephus' "Antiquities of the Jews," Book iv, Chap. 8. Josephus seems to have taken advantage of this privilege. He, being a Kohen, was nevertheless married, at the com-

An interesting case, tending to show the right of the husband, is the case of Joseph and Mary. Joseph suspected his wife of infidelity. "Then Joseph, her husband, being a just man and not willing to make her a public example, was minded to put her away privily."[1] In this case, although the reason for divorce was her supposed adultery, the right of the husband to divorce her "privily" is admitted. It would not have been necessary for Joseph to have gone before some tribunal and to have charged his wife with the crime, before being allowed to divorce her. It was a case cognizable only in the forum of his conscience.[2] Jesus himself, though generally, and especially in his ethical teachings, a follower of Hillel, herein followed the School of Shammai. The discussion between the respective champions of the two views having been carried on for a long period before the time of Jesus, it is very likely that he was entirely familiar with it. The account in Matthew[3] of his interview with the Pharisees reflects this entire Rabbinical

mand of Vespasian, to a Jewish captive, which was against the law (Josephus' "Antiquities of the Jews," Book iii, Chap. 10). At an early opportunity he divorced her, and having accompanied the Imperator Vespasian to Alexandria, he married again. After a few years he divorced his second wife, "being displeased at her conduct," and married a third wife (Josephus' "Life," Chap. 75).

[1] Matthew i, 19.
[2] The reference in the text, indicating that he might have made her a public example, alludes to the law of the woman suspected of adultery, set forth in the Book of Numbers v, 11-31, infra, p. 94.
[3] Matthew xix, 3-9.

discussion. "The Pharisees also came unto him, tempting him and saying unto him, Is it lawful for a man to put away his wife for every cause? And he answered and said unto them, Have ye not read that he which made them at the beginning made them male and female, and said, For this cause shall a man leave father and mother and shall cleave to his wife, and they twain shall be one flesh? Wherefore they are no more twain, but one flesh. What, therefore, God hath joined together, let not man put asunder. They say unto him, Why did Moses then command to give a writing of divorcement and to put her away? He saith unto them, Moses, because of the hardness of your hearts, suffered you to put away your wives, but from the beginning it was not so. And I say unto you, whosoever shall put away his wife, except it be for fornication, and shall marry another, committeth adultery; and whoso marrieth her which is put away, doth commit adultery."

The parallel passages in which the opinion of Jesus is quoted, vary somewhat in phraseology, but practically they are alike.[1] In the report of his opinion by Luke, Jesus says, "Whosoever putteth away his wife and marrieth another, committeth adultery."[2] Here no reason whatever, not even the adultery of the wife, could entitle the husband to divorce her. And this seems to have been the opinion of the zealous Paul, "And unto the married I command, yet not I, but the Lord, Let not the

[1] Matthew v, 31-32; Mark x, 2-12; Luke xvi, 18.
[2] Luke xvi, 18.

wife depart from her husband. But and if she depart, let her remain unmarried, or be reconciled to her husband. And let not the husband put away his wife."[1] Not even the unbelieving wife is to be sent away by her husband. But these lofty moral sentiments cannot be applied in their uncompromising ideality to the affairs of men, and the whole Christian world has, no doubt with regret, been obliged to sanction divorce. For until mankind has reached that state of moral perfection, when no cause will be given by either party to prompt the other to institute proceedings for divorce, it will always be more conducive to virtue and good morals to divorce ill-mated couples than to compel them against their will to remain bound by the ties of matrimony.[2]

Hillel and Aqiba, whose opinions are above quoted, were men who led an ideal life as public and private men, yet their memory has been slandered, because of their dicta on the divorce question. Their decisions in favor of the unrestricted right of the husband to divorce were opinions *ex cathedra* by judges upon a question of law. And it is a familiar fact, in modern as it was in ancient law, that it is the duty of the judges to state the law as they find it, regardless of their personal views or opinions.

[1] 1 Corinthians vii, 10-11; Romans vii, 2.
[2] Montaigne said, "We have thought to make our marriage tie stronger by taking away all means of dissolving it; but the more we have tightened the constraint, so much the more have we relaxed and detracted from the bond of will and affection."

Rabbi Elazar, who as a judge held the same opinions, said, as a moralist, "Over him who divorces the wife of his youth, even the Altar of God sheds tears." [1]

Rabbi Yoḥanan (199-279 C. E.) said,[2] "He that putteth her (his wife) away is hated of God."

Rabbi Meïr (about 150 C. E.) said,[3] "He who marries her that is divorced from her husband because of her evil conduct, is worthy of death; for he has taken a wicked woman into his house."

Rabha, a distinguished Babylonian Amora (299-352 C. E.), on being asked whether a man may divorce his wife if he finds her guilty neither of unchastity nor of any other objectionable conduct, answered, "Where a man has violated a virgin the Torah forbids him to divorce her; and if he does so he will be compelled to take her back again; but in the case about which you inquire, whatever the husband has done, is done." If he divorces her without cause he cannot be compelled to take her back again.[4] "But," continues Rabha in answer to a further question, "if his wife is living under his roof and he is harboring designs against her to divorce her (though he may exercise his right under the law), read, of him, the words of Scripture, 'Devise not evil against thy neighbor, seeing he dwelleth securely by thee.'"[5]

The moral sense which condemned the abuse of

---

[1] Talmud Babli Gittin 90 b. Alluding to Malachi ii, 13-14.
[2] Ibid.
[3] Ibid.
[4] Talmud Babli Gittin 90 a.
[5] Proverbs iii, 29.

the right to divorce found its expression in these dicta of Jesus, Elazar, Yohanan, Meïr and Rabha. What such teachers said was soon in the mouth of all men, and naturally reacted on the old law.

The old patriarchal theory was gradually modified; exceptions to the general unrestricted right of the husband gradually grew more numerous, and ere long we find the old rule practically abolished, by reason of the many exceptions to it which were recognized by the law.

But although the Rabbis did, in time, set a bar to the unlimited right of the husband, they did not seek to prevent divorce for cause or by mutual consent of the parties. The Hebrews are often somewhat maliciously called "a practical people." In no better manner did they show their practical common sense than in their divorce regulations. They did not foolishly sacrifice the realities of life to the ideal by which they were guided. They had a wholesome regard for human nature and were too practical to have false theories about it. The sacramental character that the Christian Church sought to give to marriage, and the concomitant theory of its indissolubility, never struck root among the Jews, because these theories were not in harmony with the demands of human nature and the realities of life.

The Rabbinical theory was sound and defensible. Indiscriminate exercise of the right to divorce was condemned, and moral grounds had to be given before the Rabbis gave their sanction to the proceeding. If the parties agreed to be divorced, the

Rabbis could not oppose any objection, because the mutual consent of the parties was the highest moral ground for divorce. The modern legal barbarity which yokes together in matrimony persons who mutually agree to be separated, was not countenanced by the Jewish law.[1]

[1] The most distinguished of modern sociologists, Herbert Spencer, prophesies that "A time will come when union by affection will be considered the most important, and union in the name of the law the least important, and men will hold in reprobation those conjugal unions in which union by affection is dissolved."—Herbert Spencer, "The Principles of Sociology," Vol. II, p. 410.

CHAPTER IV.

LAWS OF THE MISHNAH RESTRICTING THE HUSBAND'S RIGHT TO DIVORCE.

Modifying the Severity of the Biblical Laws of the false Accusation of Antenuptial Incontinence and of the Ravisher—The Insane Wife—The Captive—The Minor—The Formalities of Divorce Procedure—The Law of the Wife's Dowry—Denial of the Husband's Right to "Annul the Bill of Divorce"—When the Husband is *non compos mentis*—Deaf-Mute—The Culmination of these Restrictions in the Decree of Rabbi Gershom of Mayence.

THE right of the husband to divorce was, as we have seen, formally abrogated by the Mosaic law in two cases. First, where the husband had falsely charged his wife with antenuptial incontinence, and, second, in the case of the Ravisher.[1] The law relating to the false charge of antenuptial incontinence is silent as to the right of the wife to leave her husband, or to refuse to live with him. It simply states that if the charge is false, the husband shall be chastised by the elders of the city and shall pay a fine of one hundred shekels of silver to the father of the damsel and she shall be his wife, "he shall not be at liberty to put her away all his days." This apparently compels the woman to re-

[1] Deuteronomy xxii, 13-19, 28-29.

main forever with the man who, from his conduct, would probably be, of all men in the world, most odious to her. There is no positive Mishnah establishing the wife's right to leave her husband, after the false charge had been made by him, and it is only by inference that this right appears. But Philo has filled the gap by an incidental reference, which shows that the law permitted the woman to exercise her discretion and to determine whether she would continue to be his wife. He says that, when the charge of antenuptial incontinence is false, the Judges shall pronounce "what will be the most unpleasant of all things, a confirmation of the marriage, if the wife will still endure to cohabit with him; for the law permits her from her own choice to remain with him or to abandon him, and will not allow the husband any option either way, on account of the false accusation which he has brought." [1]

Another question of very great importance is neglected by the law of Deuteronomy. What shall the ravisher do, who has been compelled to marry his victim and is by law debarred from ever divorcing her, if he discovers afterwards that she is guilty of adultery? How is the rigor of this law to be reconciled with that other Biblical law, which provides that a woman guilty of adultery cannot remain with her husband? Josephus supplies the information required on this point, showing how the law had been modified by Rabbinical decisions.

[1] Philo, "Of Special Laws Relating to Adultery, etc.," Chap. 14, Yonge's Edition, Vol. III, pp. 323-4.

He says, "if the damsel (charged with antenuptial incontinence) is declared innocent, let her live with her husband that accused her, and let him not have the power thereafter to put her away, unless she give him so grave cause and such as can in no way be contradicted."[1] Here then, the rigor of the law, that "he shall not have the power to put her away all his days," is modified, to prevent the greater immorality of compelling a man to live with an adulteress, when she is well known to be such. And the Mishnah, to which Josephus no doubt alludes, says very distinctly, that if after the marriage she commits adultery, she must be divorced; for it is written in the law "unto him shall she be a *wife*," that is, one who is fit and worthy to be so called. The adulteress therefore could not have been intended thereby.[2] A distinction is made between the case of the seducer and the ravisher, the punishment of the latter being greater. In addition to the greater pecuniary liability of the ravisher, he, as was shown above, was punished by having his marriage with the woman whom he had wronged, made indissoluble. The Biblical law provides that the seducer may, if the father of the damsel refuses to give her to him as a wife, compound the offense by paying a fine;[3] and the Mishnah properly concludes that when the crime was committed with the consent of the woman, the punishment should not be severe; hence, although the seducer, in compli-

[1] Josephus' "Antiquities," Book iv, Chap. 8.
[2] Mishnah Kethuboth iii, 4-5.
[3] Exodus xxii, 16-17.

ance with the letter of the law, had to marry the woman whom he had seduced, he could, if he chose, divorce her.[1]

The Mishnah provides for another exception, which commends itself to reason. If the woman for any reason whatsoever has religious disqualifications which cannot be removed, the ravisher need not marry her, although he is obliged to pay to her father not only the fifty shekels provided by the Biblical law, but also punitive damages, to be estimated according to her rank, station and condition in life, for the injury done to her and for her shame and suffering. Philo seems to have been of the opinion that the ravisher, as well as the seducer, could in any case refuse to marry the damsel, and was obliged merely to pay a fine and provide her with a dowry for another husband; but that, if he consent to take her as his wife, he must marry her at once, without delay, in order that the mishap may be comforted by a firm marriage, which nothing but death shall disturb.[2] But this was not the law. The ravisher cannot refuse to marry her if she is willing. The Mishnah says: "The ravisher must drink out of his polluted vessel," and even if the woman whom he has ravished is afflicted with personal blemishes, he must marry her and keep her as a wife forever.[3]

While, on the one hand, the Mishnah has

[1] Mishnah Kethuboth iii, 4.
[2] Philo, "Of Special Laws Relating to Adultery, etc.," Chap. 11, Yonge's Edition, Vol. III, pp. 320-321.
[3] Mishnah Kethuboth iii, 5.

somewhat modified the unyielding severity of the
Mosaic law, in permitting the slanderer or the ravisher to divorce the woman whom he has been
obliged to marry, it has also, on the other hand,
extended the number of cases in which there is an
absolute prohibition of divorce.

The Mosaic law did not, except in the two
cases above mentioned, prevent the husband from
divorcing his wife under any and all circumstances;
but the oral law furnished three exceptions to this
general privilege. It provided, in the first place,
that where the wife had become insane, she could
not be divorced. In this case the woman being
unable to take care of herself, might become the
prey of evil men, and hence the Doctors of the
Mishnah deemed it proper to forbid the divorce.[1]
But as this was in derogation of the ancient right
of the husband, the Rabbis sought to find Biblical
sanction for it. It was not enough for them to
say, we deem it against public policy or against
good morals; they had to find some Biblical
authority for their innovation. Rabbi Yannai
(about 220 C. E.) explained it thus: The Torah
says "he shall give it (the Bill of Divorce) into
her hands," *i. e.*, she must be a rational creature,
capable of receiving it. In the college of Rabbi
Ishmael another reason was given. The Torah
says, "and he sends her from his house," *i. e.*, it
refers to one who, being sent away, will not return;
but a demented person has no sense of shame
and will probably go back to her husband's

---

[1] Mishnah Yebamoth xiv, 1.

house. The Bible does not allow such a one to be divorced.[1]

But it seems that although some of the Rabbis forbade the divorce of an insane wife, others permitted it,[2] on the principle that the ancient legal right of the husband could not be abrogated.

In the next place it was decided that the wife could not be divorced while she was in captivity. If she had been taken captive in war, or by a band of Bedouins, it was the duty of the husband to ransom her, and he could not escape this obligation by sending her a Bill of Divorce, even though he also sent her the amount of her dowry and bade her use it to ransom herself.[3]

Finally, it was decided that the minor wife, who is so young as not to be able to understand or to take care of her Get or Bill of Divorce, could not be divorced.[4] It is not unusual in Oriental countries to give girls in marriage at a very tender age, and the above provision was dictated by principles of the soundest common sense.

The theoretical right of the husband to divorce at his pleasure was further modified by the formalities attending the preparation and delivery of the Bill of Divorce. The numerous rules and regulations incident to the procedure in divorce com-

[1] Talmud Babli Yebamoth 113 b.
[2] Maimonides' Treatise Gerushin x, 23.
[3] Mishnah Kethuboth iv, 9. But if after having been ransomed she is again made captive, he is no longer obliged to ransom her. Talmud Babli Kethuboth 52 a. Maimonides' Treatise Ishuth xiv, 19.
[4] Ibid.

pelled the husband to seek the help of one learned in the law to assist him in divorcing his wife, and thus the act became a quasi-judicial one. Although the duties of the person thus consulted by the husband were ministerial, he was obliged to be well versed in the law,[1] and was expected to use every effort to reconcile the parties, unless sufficient reason appeared for the divorce.[2]

The law compelling payment of the wife's dowry when she was divorced also acted as a check upon the husband's abuse of his right. It was an old Biblical institution and was probably pro-Mosaic;[3] and by its means some of the difficulties that have been suggested in reference to two other Biblical laws can be explained. It has been asked,[4] if the law allowed divorce at the pleasure of the husband, what is the sense of the law of the accusation of antenuptial incontinence?[5] The husband would certainly not go through the unpleasant formalities of a public accusation of his wife, if he could, without question, rid himself of her by a Bill of Divorce. The answer to this is found in the law of the wife's dowry. By a contract, expressed or implied, the husband secured to his wife, in the

[1] Talmud Babli Qiddushin 6 a.
[2] For procedure in divorce see Chapters xii–xiv.
[3] Infra, p. 111. The Egyptians had a similar law by which the dowry of the wife was inalienable, and was payable to her on being divorced. Letourneau, " Evolution of Marriage and the Family," p. 177.
[4] Commentary of Naḥmani to Deuteronomy xxiv, 1-4, and xxii, 13-19.
[5] Deuteronomy xxii, 13-19.

event of his death or divorce, a certain sum of money, and also, by later law, the return to her of the property which she brought to him upon her marriage. If the wife was found guilty of ante-nuptial incontinence, she was put to death; but if the husband divorced her without public inquiry, she was entitled to her dowry and to the return of the property which she brought to her husband at her marriage. It was, therefore, a pecuniary advantage to the husband to get rid of his wife by a public accusation. As this, however, was liable to be abused by an unscrupulous man, who would not hesitate to prefer a false charge against the wife of whom he desired to be rid, without satisfying her just property claims, it was provided by law that the husband preferring such a false charge was obliged to keep his wife and could not divorce her "all her days."[1]

Another limitation upon the husband's ancient rights was the decree of Rabban Gamaliel, which deprived him of the power of "annulling the Bill of Divorce." According to ancient law, the husband, after he had sent off the messenger with the Bill of Divorce for his wife, could summon witnesses and in their presence declare his Bill of Divorce or Get null and void; and this, although neither the messenger nor the wife was present.[2] The dangerous consequences of this power were obvious. The woman receiving the Get from the messenger, and considering herself divorced, might

[1] Deuteronomy xxii, 19.
[2] Mishnah Gittin iv, 2.

be married to another man, only to discover afterwards that her former husband had annulled his Get, whereby her second marriage became void, she became an adulteress and her issue by her second husband illegitimate. This power of the husband was a survival of the immemorial right of the patriarch to do as he pleased with his own, bound by no other law than the dictates of his conscience; and it continued in force until Rabban Gamaliel the Elder, who was Chief of the Sanhedrin during the reign of Agrippa (about 40 C.E.), decided that the husband no longer had the right to annul the Get in the absence of the messenger or of the wife.[1] The authority of Rabban Gamaliel was frequently questioned, until, about one hundred years later, his great-grandson Rabban Simon (III) ben Gamaliel (Nasi from about 140-164 C.E.) decided that the decree of Rabban Gamaliel must be accepted as law, and that it was beyond the power of later Rabbis to set aside the decrees of so eminent a tribunal as that over which Rabban Gamaliel presided. He maintained that marriage was contracted subject to all Biblical and Rabbinical laws in force at the time of its solemnization, and as the Court of Rabban Gamaliel had rendered an opinion on this question, every man was presumed to know that if he married and divorced his wife, he had no power to "annul his Get." This having been the law at the time of his marriage, he was bound to know and obey it.[2]

[1] Mishnah Gittin iv, 2.
[2] Talmud Babli Gittin 33 a.

50   THE JEWISH LAW OF DIVORCE.

The restrictions thus imposed by the law upon the husband's theoretical right to divorce his wife whenever he pleased, were further increased by other Rabbinical decisions.

WHEN HUSBAND IS INSANE.—The insane man is incapable of exercising legal rights or performing legal acts, and could therefore not give a Bill of Divorce to his wife, or order it to be given for him.[1] If he was only temporarily deranged, in a delirium, or stupidly intoxicated with strong drink so as to be deprived of his ordinary faculties, he was considered incapacitated for the time being from performing any legal act.[2]

The case of one who is stricken with cardiacos[3] is analogous in law to the case of the insane person. It seems that this disease disqualified a person from the performance of any legal act, so that if one while in the throes of this disease ordered a Get to be written for his wife, it was considered "as though he had said nothing." He was not deemed competent to give expression to a rational purpose.[4]

DEAF-MUTE.—One who was deaf and dumb was not deemed to be quite as unsound as an idiot or an

[1] Mishnah Yebamoth xiv, 1.
[2] Talmud Babli Gittin 67 b. Maimonides' Treatise Gerushin ii, 14.
[3] The exact nature of this disease is not known. From the term used in the Mishnah to describe it, it seems to have been some cardiac affection, and was perhaps accompanied by some very abnormal physical condition which led the Rabbis to believe that the person so stricken was deprived of his intellectual faculties.
[4] Mishnah Gittin vii, 1.

insane person, and was therefore not entirely incapacitated from the performance of certain legal acts. But, having been deprived of two of the most important means of understanding others and giving expression to his own thoughts, he was under certain legal disabilities. He could not be a witness in legal proceedings[1] and he was classed with infants, being, in the eye of the law, only able to exercise legal rights over certain trifling matters in and about his household,[2] but not considered as endowed with ordinary legal responsibilities.[3]

If a deaf and dumb person desired to be married, he could perform the ceremony of espousing his wife by signs. This marriage ceremony was not strictly valid according to the Biblical law, but it was sanctioned, owing to the necessities of the case, by Rabbinical law. It followed, therefore, that having espoused his wife by signs, he could divorce her by signs, and might express his intention to the scribe and the witnesses by gesture and pantomime.[4] But if the husband who had been entirely sound and in possession of all his senses at his marriage, afterwards became deaf-mute, the law did not allow him to divorce his wife; the marriage having been entered into under such circumstances and under such forms, as to be binding, could only be dissolved " according to the Law of Moses and Israel." [5]

[1] Talmud Babli Gittin 71 a.
[2] Mishnah Gitin v, 7.
[3] Mishnah Baba Qama viii, 5.
[4] Mishnah Yebamoth xiv, 1.
[5] Mishnah Yebamoth, Ibid.

THE DECREE OF RABBI GERSHOM.—These numerous qualifications of the theoretical right of the husband to give the Bill of Divorce to his wife whenever it pleased him to do so, resulted in gradually eliminating from the popular mind the notion that such a right existed. Men had become so accustomed to go to the Rabbi, who was both spiritual leader and judge, when they wished to divorce their wives, that they eventually forgot that, by ancient common law, they were entitled to give the Bill of Divorce without the Rabbi's sanction.

In the beginning of the eleventh century of the Common Era, the theoretical right of the husband, which for centuries theretofore had ceased to exist in practice, was formally declared to be at an end. This was done by a decree issued by Rabbi Gershom ben Yehudah (about 1025 C.E.), who presided over a Sanhedrin convened at Mayence.[1] The substance of this decree is thus stated:—

"To assimilate the right of the woman to the right of the man, it is ordained that even as the man does not put away his wife except of his own free will, so shall the woman not be put away except by her own consent."[2] Always excepting the cases where good cause has been shown by either husband or wife why the marriage should be dissolved against the will of the other.[3]

This decree was accepted as law by the Jews of

[1] Commentary of Rabbi Moses Isserles to Eben Haëzer cxix, 6.
[2] Responsa Asheri 42, 1.
[3] Commentary of Rabbi Moses Isserles to Eben Haëzer cxix, 6.

the countries represented in the Sanhedrin, and afterwards by all who acknowledged the authority of the Shulḥan Arukh;[1] but Maimonides, who compiled his Code about one hundred and fifty years after this decree (1180 C.E.), ignores it entirely and seems to have been unaware of its existence.

This decree of Rabbi Gershom, and his other decree abolishing polygamy, were remarkable because of their revolutionary character. It was a principle of interpretation that the things which are expressly permitted in the Bible, cannot be prohibited by Rabbinical authority.[2] The authority of the Sanhedrin of Rabbi Gershom was self-constituted, and its decrees in defiance of immemorial custom, and Biblical law, are illustrative of the intellectual independence of the Rabbis, more especially when it is remembered that they were promulgated amidst the surrounding darkness of the Middle Ages.

[1] In the case of Moss vs. Smith, 1 Manning & Granger 228, decided in the Court of Common Pleas at London in 1840, this question was mooted.

[2] Turë Zahab sub Ḥoshen Mishpat ii.

CHAPTER V.

THE WIFE'S RIGHT TO SUE FOR DIVORCE.

The Germ of the Wife's Right Found in the Bible—Jurisdiction of the Courts to Compel the Husband to Grant the Bill of Divorce—The Question of Duress—The Acts of non-Jewish Courts—The Wife could Sue for Divorce, but could not Give a Bill of Divorce to her Husband—Influence of Roman Law during the last Days of the Jewish State.

THAT the Biblical law has neglected to make the rights as well as the duties of husband and wife entirely reciprocal, and to provide for the wife's right to sue for divorce, has been a source of frequent comment. The reason for the silence of the law on this question is, however, obvious. In a state of society where the husband and father was practically a sovereign in dealing with his own, the case of a wife suing for divorce could not have occurred to the lawgivers, because there was no forum in which she could obtain redress. The wife was a part of the husband's *familia*, and looked to her lord and master for her law.[1] He, as the representative of the household, very likely appeared in the council of the Elders and Heads of the Houses to discuss and decide questions affecting the common weal, but hardly to discuss the internal affairs of his household.

[1] Genesis iii, 16.

The germ of the wife's right to sue for divorce does, however, exist in the Pentateuch. "And if a man sell his daughter to be a maid-servant, she shall not go out as the men-servants do. If she please not her master who betrothed her to himself, then shall he let her be redeemed; to sell her unto another, he shall have no power, seeing he hath dealt deceitfully with her. And if he have betrothed her unto his son, he shall deal with her after the manner of daughters. If he take him another wife, her food, her raiment and her duty of marriage shall he not diminish. And if he do not these three unto her, then shall she go out free without money."[1] Under this law a father had the right to sell his daughter as a bondwoman, whereby she left his household and entered that of her master. As soon as she was elevated from the position of a bondwoman, and betrothed to her master's son, she was entitled to certain rights. She could not be sold again, and could, as a wife, demand food, raiment, and conjugal rights, of her husband. If he refused these, she could "go out free."[2] But as it is not in the nature of things that a bond-

---

[1] Exodus xxi, 7–11.

[2] Likewise, in the case of the woman taken captive in war, who has been made the wife of her captor, the law says that, after she has been *married*, "if thou have no delight in her, then thou shalt let her go whither she will, but thou shalt not sell her at all for money, thou shalt not make merchandise of her, because thou hast humbled her" (Deuteronomy xxi, 14). In this case, the captive, who by the laws of war became a bondwoman and who had been elevated to the dignity of wifehood, *could not, after the marriage had been consummated, be sold by her husband*.

woman should go out free from the power of her master, whenever she believed herself entitled to do so, the inference seems to be that she could appeal to some lawful authority, perhaps the Elders of the City, to protect her rights, or to secure her freedom on proving that her rights had been withheld.

The Mekhilta[1] hints at such a state of things. "If the husband does not provide for his wife (who had been his bondwoman) in accordance with the law, then shall she go out free without money, *but not without a Bill of Divorce.*" As the giving of a Bill of Divorce, for the husband's neglect of his legal duties, could only be enforced by some lawful authority, it follows that the woman must have been entitled to appeal to such authority to maintain her rights against her husband.

This tradition in the Mekhilta also indicated. that the granting of the Bill of Divorce was a very old custom in Israel, and necessary to dissolve a lawful marriage.

Here then is probably a case, under the patriarchal system, of a woman suing at law for her freedom from the power of her master. It is fair to presume that if the bondwoman had this right, the freeborn wife had an equal, if not a better right.

This is the germ of the modern theory that the relation existing between the married couple is founded on contract. By virtue of the position that the woman assumed in the husband's household, she obtained certain rights against him. He

[1] Mishpatim, Section 3.

having taken her into his *manus*, the law imposed upon him certain obligations towards her. The next step probably was, the recognition of the wife as plaintiff before the Elders of the City or the Heads of the Houses, in case the husband failed in his duty towards her, and the infliction of some penalty for his transgression. This penalty very likely consisted of a fine or a levy on some of his property for her sustenance. Eventually (at first no doubt in flagrant cases) the judges compelled the husband to release her entirely by giving her a bill of divorce.

The right to compel the husband to give a bill of divorce to his wife, may well have appeared doubtful to these ancient judges who were ingrained with the theory of the absolute right of the head of the house to deal as he pleased with his own; and the judge or the Council of Elders who first exercised this right were no doubt looked upon as usurpers of authority. But the right existed at a very early period, and the courts had the power to compel the husband's consent to a divorce by the infliction of corporal punishment, usually thirty-nine stripes.[1]

The objection to the Bill of Divorce thus given under order of the court was that it was given under duress. The law required that the husband should act as a free agent,[2] and if he granted the divorce to his wife while under fear of punishment for disobeying the order of the court, he could not be said to be acting of his own free will.[3] The

[1] Mishnah Erakhin v, 6.
[2] Mishnah Yebamoth xiv, 1.
[3] Mishnah Gittin ix, 8.

question thus raised went to the very heart of the right of the courts to interpret the written law. As long as the woman had no right to be heard against her husband, such a question could not arise; but once having admitted the right of a woman to appear as plaintiff, the courts were bound to assume the authority to enforce their decrees against the husband as defendant.[1] Here they were met with the objection above stated, that no Get was valid unless it was the free act of the husband, and the right of the court, therefore, to enforce its own decrees was directly in issue. Being unwilling to usurp authority, and feeling at the same time that the necessity of the case justified their position, they evaded the issue by a very neat bit of reasoning. They said, in substance, "We do not compel the husband to give this Get against his will. We assume that every man intends to act according to law. The law says that this woman shall receive a Get, and it therefore becomes the duty of the husband to give it to her.[2] His refusal to do so, is the result of an evil disposition which prompts him to act contrary to law. It is this evil disposition which is forcing him to do that which is wrong. It is therefore both our right and our duty to help him to get rid of his evil disposition, so that he may do that which the law directs. We accomplish this purpose by punishing him for disobeying our decree and until he acts in accordance with it.[3] When he has been sufficiently pun-

[1] Mishnah Erakhin v, 6.
[2] Talmud Babli Baba Bathra 48 a.
[3] Talmud Babli Yebamoth 106 a.

ished, his evil disposition will leave him and he will be able, as a free agent, to give the divorce according to law."[1]

This argument justified the Jewish courts in enforcing their decrees in divorce against the husband; but the Rabbis refused to apply it for the purpose of validating Bills of Divorce which were prepared in the courts of the Heathen (Romans).[2] In all cases, where the non-Jewish Courts conducted the divorce proceedings of a Jewish couple, the Rabbis declared their act to be null and void.[3] Although the Jewish authorities readily submitted all questions affecting civil rights and contracts to the courts of the Gentiles, they always refused to recognize their authority in religious matters. Divorce was a quasi-religious act among the Jews; the woman was said to be married and divorced "according to the law of Moses and Israel." The Bill of Divorce was peculiar to the Jews and other nations did not make use of it in divorce proceedings;[4] for these reasons the interference of non-Jewish courts in matters of marriage and divorce was deemed a usurpation of authority even when both the parties voluntarily submitted to its jurisdiction. But in cases where the court of the Gentiles exercised merely an ancillary jurisdiction for the purpose of enforcing a decree of the Jewish court, its action was recognized as valid and bind-

[1] Maimonides' Treatise Gerushin ii, 20, inferred from Talmud Babli Baba Bathra 48 a.
[2] Mishnah Gittin ix, 8.
[3] Idem i, 5.
[4] Talmud Yerushalmi Qiddushin sub Mishnah i, 1 (48 a).

ing, because it was merely the executive agent of the Jewish court and did not assume any original jurisdiction.[1] Hence the Mishnah states, "if the heathen tribunal forces the husband to give a Get, saying to him, 'Do thou that which the Jewish tribunal has ordered thee to do,' the divorce is valid."[2]

Although in course of time the wife was recognized as a plaintiff in divorce proceedings and could obtain a decree of the Court to compel her husband to divorce her, the law always supposed that the husband was giving the divorce of his own free will and accord. By means of this legal fiction no violence was done to the letter of the old law, and the theory of the husband's exclusive right to give the divorce was apparently maintained; yet the divorce given by the husband under order of the court, at the suit of his wife, was as much a judicial divorce as any modern proceeding of such a nature. The woman was never entitled to divorce her husband at Jewish law. Such an act would have been in opposition to the fundamental theory that divorce was the exclusive right of the husband, and although, as was shown above, this exclusive right was modified in favor of the wife, the old forms were always used and the idea of the bill of divorce given by the wife to her husband was impossible to the Jewish legal mind.

Josephus records that two ladies of the royal

[1] During the latter days of the Jewish Commonwealth, when the Roman power was established in Palestine, it was not unusual for the Jewish Courts to call in the aid of the Roman Courts to enforce their decrees.
[2] Mishnah Gittin ix, 8.

THE WIFE'S RIGHT TO SUE FOR DIVORCE. 61

house of Herod the Great divorced their husbands by sending them a Get. These were Salome, the sister of Herod,[1] and Herodias, his grand-daughter.[2] In both cases, Josephus notes his disapproval, and he declares these things to have been done in contempt of the Jewish law. Judea was at that time, and had been for two hundred years, a vassal of Rome. Roman influence made itself felt, especially among the upper classes, and it is very likely that these high-born dames were supersaturated with Roman culture.

The Roman law,[3] at the time of Herod allowed women to divorce their husbands, and it was under this influence that the divorces were given by the women of Herod's family.[4]

This departure from the Jewish law by the Herodian family had its influence on the people and, no doubt, found imitators. It seems to have attracted the attention of Jesus, and he strongly condemned it, saying, "if a woman shall put away her husband and be married to another she com-

[1] Josephus' "Antiquities of the Jews," Book xv, Chap. 11.
[2] Idem, Book xviii, Chap. 7.
[3] Institutes of Gaius, I Sect. 137.
[4] The repudiation at Roman Law was valid, although without cause, so that it was not necessary to acquaint the other party with the change in his or her condition. If the wife repudiated her husband in the presence of witnesses, the marriage was dissolved without notice to the husband (Code of Justinian, Book v, Title xvii, Constitution 6), although it was considered proper to give such notice (Digest, Book xxiv, Title ii, Fragment ii, Section iii). The wife who was *in manu* could not divorce her husband.

mitteth adultery;"[1] and this was an exact statement of the Jewish law. The practice which is thus condemned existed for a time under the Roman influence, but after the destruction of the Temple it was heard of no more.

The right of the wife to demand a divorce from her husband having once been established, the causes for which that right could be exercised gradually became more numerous. The purpose of the marriage was fulfilled only when the conjugal parties were in entire harmony. At first, the law considered few causes of sufficient consequence to entitle the wife to a divorce. Under the shadow of the ancient patriarchal power it was difficult for public law to attempt to regulate the relation of the husband and wife; but the Mishnah records numerous causes for which the wife could sue for divorce.

[1] Mark x, 12.

CHAPTER VI.

CAUSES ENTITLING THE WIFE TO A DIVORCE UNDER TALMUDIC LAW.

False Accusation of Antenuptial Incontinence—Refusal of Conjugal Rights—Impotence—Vow of Celibacy—Priest's Wife—Physical Blemishes, etc.—Leprosy—Non-support—Restricting Wife's Lawful Freedom—Wife-beating—Desertion—Apostasy—Licentiousness—Divorce of Betrothed Wife.

HUSBAND'S FALSE CHARGE OF ANTENUPTIAL INCONTINENCE.—Perhaps one of the most ancient causes for which the wife could demand a divorce was, the false accusation of antenuptial incontinence. Philo has recorded the fact that the woman was entitled, if she pleased, to be released from the marriage with the man who by his false accusation had become odious to her.[1]

REFUSAL OF CONJUGAL RIGHTS.—The Torah says, "her food, her raiment and her duty of marriage shall he not diminish."[2] This "duty of marriage" was obligatory on the husband, and its refusal constituted a good ground of divorce. There could not be any decree compelling cohabitation, and the courts, therefore, did not hesitate to give the

[1] Philo, "Of Special Laws Relating to Adultery, etc." Chap. 14, Yonge's Edition, Vol. III, pp. 323-4; supra, p. 42.
[2] Exodus xxi, 10.

woman other redress.[1] A fixed period was given to the husband to reconsider his determination and if he had bound himself by a vow, to enable him to be absolved therefrom. According to the School of Hillel, one week, according to the School of Shammai, two weeks,[2] and according to the later Schools, four weeks[3] were allowed him. The time having elapsed, he was obliged either to restore her conjugal rights or to give her a bill of divorce.[4]

Mohammed adopted this provision of the Jewish law, and gave the husband a longer time for consideration. "They who vow to abstain from their wives are allowed to wait four months, but if they go back from their vow, verily, God is gracious and merciful; and if they resolve on divorce, God is he who heareth and knoweth."[5]

The Jewish wife was at liberty to exercise her option either to demand a divorce after the period fixed by law had elapsed, or to remain with her husband. In the latter case, if he continued refractory, he was fined three denarii weekly,[6] which were allowed to accumulate and were added to her dowry, becoming, like the latter, a lien on his estate. When the refusal of the husband was due to sickness or temporary impediment, he was allowed six

[1] Mishnah Nedarim ix, 4.
[2] Mishnah Kethuboth v, 6.
[3] Maimonides' Treatise Ishuth x, 23.
[4] Mishnah Kethuboth v, 6. If the bridegroom refused to consummate the marriage after betrothal, the bride was entitled to a divorce (Mishnah Kethuboth xiii, 5).
[5] Koran (Sale's Translation), Sûra 2.
[6] Mishnah Kethuboth v, 7.

months' time to be cured. If after this time he was found incurable the wife was entitled to a divorce.[1] But if the disease or impediment was in its nature curable, additional time was given, and the divorce was not decreed until the possibilities of curing it had been exhausted.[2]

IMPOTENCE OF THE HUSBAND.—Under an old rule of law the woman who charged her husband with impotence was entitled to a divorce, without being compelled to prove the charge.[3] But as this led to abuse and fraud, a later Mishnah made it obligatory on the court to attempt to reconcile the parties before compelling the husband to divorce her.[4]

The natural desire to have children to support the declining years of the parents, was elevated to the dignity of a quasi-legal right.[5] If the marriage was childless after ten years of cohabitation and the wife charged the husband with physical impotence, she was entitled to a divorce.[6] If there were cross-charges, each charging the other with impotence, Rabbi Ami decided that the presumption was always in favor of the woman and the burden of proof rested on the husband;[7] for it was a presumption upon which the Rabbis constantly acted, that in matters affecting husband and wife, the

[1] Maimonides' Treatise Ishuth xiv, 7.
[2] Beër Heteb to Eben Haëzer 76, Sect. 11.
[3] Mishnah Nedarim xi, 12.
[4] Ibid.
[5] Talmud Babli Yebamoth 65 b.
[6] Ibid.
[7] Talmud Babli Yebamoth 65 a.

latter would not venture to assert a fact in the presence of her husband unless it were true.¹

WIFE'S VOW OF ABSTENTION FROM CONNUBIAL INTERCOURSE.—Under an old law, the wife who vowed to abstain from connubial intercourse was entitled to a divorce from her husband.² The object of marriage having been defeated, the woman was entitled to a divorce, even though her husband was willing to maintain the mere form of marriage. But as it was a double hardship in this case, for the husband to be compelled to divorce his wife and at the same time pay her the Kethubah, when he was perfectly innocent of any wrong, a partial remedy was provided by the later Mishnah. Under the Mosaic Law, the husband had the right to annul the vows of his wife;³ the Rabbis therefore decided that in this case the husband could annul her vow so far as it related to him. If, after the vow had been annulled by him, the woman persisted in her resolution, she was no longer entitled to a divorce, and the husband was released from the payment of the Kethubah, if he chose to divorce her.⁴ The fault in this case clearly lay with the woman, who attempted by her vow of abstention to annul her vows of marriage.

PRIEST'S WIFE WHO HAS BECOME UNCLEAN.—Another instance in which the wife could by her own will establish the cause for which the husband was compelled to divorce her, was the case of the wife

[1] Talmud Babli Gittin, 64 b.
[2] Mishnah Nedarim xi, 12.
[3] Numbers xxx, 8-9.
[4] Talmud Babli Kethuboth 63 b.

of a priest who went before the court declaring that she was unclean, *i. e.*, that she was no longer fit to live with him, an account of his holiness of station. Upon her statement and without requiring further proof, the court compelled the husband to divorce her;[1] but in order to prevent abuse of this privilege, the later law compelled the wife to properly prove her case, before she was entitled to her divorce.[2]

PHYSICAL BLEMISHES, ETC.—Rabbi Simon ben Gamaliel (Nasi from 140-164 C. E.) decided that where the husband was afflicted with a serious disease, such as leprosy or πολύπος,[3] or where he was engaged in some malodorous business, such as gathering dog's dung, smelting copper or tanning hides, that the wife was entitled to a divorce,[4] and it made no difference that these objections were known to her before the marriage. But if she had especially covenanted before her marriage not to take advantage of these objections for the purpose of suing for divorce, she was estopped from urging them for such purpose.[5] In the case, however, where the husband was afflicted with leprosy, the divorce was enforced by the court without respect to the wishes of the parties, because connubial intercourse would "unnerve" him.[6]

REFUSAL TO SUPPORT.—Among the first duties

[1] Mishnah Nedarim xi, 12.
[2] Ibid.
[3] Some offensive catarrhal affection (cancer?).
[4] Mishnah Kethuboth vii, 9.
[5] Ibid, 10.
[6] Ibid.

imposed upon the husband was that of properly maintaining or supporting his wife, *i. e.*, giving her food, raiment and shelter, in accordance with her station in life.[1] The minimum was prescribed by law, and consisted of those absolute essentials without which life would be a misery. When a man was so poor that he could not even give his wife the absolute necessaries of life, he was obliged, on her application, to give her a divorce,[2] and her Kethubah remained a lien on all his after acquired goods, until he had paid it in full. The later Rabbis went further, and said that he who had only one day's food would be compelled to give her as much of it as was necessary for her support;[3] if he had lands, she could take the usufruct for her support, and in case this was not sufficient, she could take the land itself; and the husband was obliged to sell it to support her.[4] Still others went to the length of saying that he must hire out as a day laborer in order to fulfil the obligations of the Kethubah and support his wife;[5] and in case the husband was rich he was not only compelled to give his wife the common necessaries of life, but was obliged to support her in accordance with his wealth and station.[6] If the husband refused to support his wife, the court made an order for her

[1] Mishnah Kethuboth v, 8, 9.
[2] Talmud Babli Kethuboth 63 a.
[3] Opinion of Rabbi Solomon ben Adreth cited in Rabbi Isserles' gloss to Eben Haëzer lxx, 3.
[4] Ibid.
[5] Ibid.
[6] Mishnah Kethuboth v, 9.

support, and if he then refused to obey the order of the court and would not even give her the necessaries of life, or if he had nothing and was not willing to make an effort to earn enough to maintain her, she was entitled to a divorce.¹ When this question arose in the Schools of Babylonia,² Rab or Abba Areka (175–247 C. E.) was of the opinion that she was entitled to a divorce immediately, for, said he, "the woman has the right to say, I cannot dwell in the same cage with a serpent." But the opinion of his contemporary Mar Samuel bar Abba (160–257 C. E.), commonly called Samuel, prevailed, that the Court must first order him to support her and upon his refusal to do so, she is entitled to a divorce.³

RESTRICTIONS ON THE WIFE'S LIBERTY.—It was the privilege of the husband, under the Mosaic Law, to annul the rash or improvident vows of his wife and absolve her from their obligation,⁴ and his failure to do so was, in some cases, considered tantamount to a severance of the marriage relation. Where the wife by a vow deprived herself of any right or privilege, and the husband did not absolve her, as he might have done, she was entitled to a divorce.⁵

The presumption in this case was that the husband having neglected to annul her vow, was satis-

¹ Talmud Babli Kethuboth 77 a.
² Ibid.
³ Some of the later Rabbis adhered to the opinion of Rab. Beër Heteb to Eben Haëzer cliv, 3.
⁴ Numbers xxx, 8–9.
⁵ Mishnah Kethuboth vii, 2–5.

fied with it. This placed him in the same position as though he had made such a vow, laying certain restrictions upon his wife, and for this she was entitled to a divorce.[1]

Among the cases cited in the Mishnah are vows that she shall not eat a certain kind of fruit or wear a certain ornament; that she shall not enter her father's house, or a house of mourning or rejoicing. Rabbi Kahana (about 400 C.E.) includes the case where he vows that she shall not borrow any cooking utensil of her neighbors, "for this will give her a bad reputation,"[2] and Rabbi Simon ben Gamaliel (about 150 C.E.) decided that where the husband interdicted his wife, by a vow, from the performance of any kind of work, thereby condemning her to live in idleness, she was entitled to a divorce, because idleness might result in mental aberration.[3]

The effect of these decisions, generally stated, was, that when the husband treated his wife tyrannically and sought to deprive her of her lawful freedom, she was entitled to a divorce. Under the later law, she was even privileged to refuse to allow her mother-in-law or other persons to come to live in the same house with her if she feared that they would annoy her, on the broad principle that this was an infringement on her right of personal liberty.[4]

WIFE BEATING.—All systems of law, ancient as

[1] Talmud Babli Kethuboth 72 a.
[2] Ibid.
[3] Mishnah Kethuboth v, 5.
[4] Maimonides' Treatise Ishuth xiii, 14.

well as modern, gave the husband the right to moderately chastise his wife for her misconduct.[1] The Koran says: "Those whose perverseness you are apprehensive of, rebuke; and remove them into separate apartments and chastise them."[2]

The opinion of Rabbi Isserles, as reported in Eben Haëzer, Cap. 154, Sec.3, sums up the ancient Jewish law and its bearing on the question. He says, "A man who beats his wife commits a sin, as though he had beaten his neighbor, and if he persists in his conduct the court may castigate him and excommunicate him and place him under oath to discontinue this conduct; if he refuses to obey the order of court, they will compel him to divorce his wife at once (though some are of the opinion that he should be warned once or twice) because it is not customary or proper for Jews to beat their wives; it is a custom of the heathen. This is the law where he is in fault; but if she curses him or insults his parents, some are of the opinion that he may beat her, and others say even if she is a bad woman he may not beat her; but I am of the first opinion. If it is not known who began the quarrel the husband is not permitted to testify that she was the aggressor; for all women are presumed to be innocent."

To this opinion is appended the opinion of the Rabbi Jacob Weil, that "he who beats his wife is in greater fault than he who beats his neighbor, for

[1] Novels of Justinian cxvii, Sec. 14. Blackstone's Commentaries i, 144.
[2] Koran (Sale's Translation), Sûra 4.

he is not obliged to protect the honor of his neighbor, but he is obliged to protect the honor of his wife; he must honor her more than himself; she rises with him but does not descend with him;[1] she was given him as a companion for life and not for misery,[2] and his punishment for ill-treating her is greater than for ill-treating his neighbor, for she trusts in him and confidingly rests under his roof."

DESERTION.—The wife was entitled to a divorce in cases which amount to a technical desertion, in the modern sense of the term. It must be premised that if the husband deserted his wife and was beyond the jurisdiction of the court, he could not be compelled to give his wife a Get, and even though he remained away and was never heard of again, the wife was not freed from the bonds of matrimony; for, in the first place, it was always the husband who was presumed to grant the divorce, although it was done under the order of the court, at the suit of the wife. There is no proceeding known at Jewish law, analogous to a modern suit for divorce on the ground of the husband's desertion, in which the divorce is granted judicially in the absence of the husband and without his consent. There is, in the second place, no presumption of death from absence after a certain number of years and, therefore, the woman who was deserted by her husband remained a wife forever, as she had received no Get from him and as

[1] Talmud Babli Kethuboth 60 a.
[2] Talmud Babli Kethuboth 61 a.

she could not be presumed to be his widow. She was known as the Egunah (the chained one).[1]

But there are cases at Jewish law which may technically be termed cases of desertion, in which the wife was entitled to receive a Get from her husband *before* he left the jurisdiction of the court. Where she, living in a foreign country, desired to remove to Palestine, or, living in Palestine, desired to remove to the city of Jerusalem, and her husband refused to allow her to remove, or to accompany her, he was, at her instance, compelled by the court to give her a Get; or if she was living in Jerusalem and he desired her to remove to some other city in Palestine, or, if living elsewhere in Palestine, he desired her to remove to some foreign country, and she refused to accompany him, she could, if she feared that he would desert her, appeal to the court, who would compel him to give her a bill of divorce before leaving.[2]

This divorce for desertion was granted only in the above cases, and did not apply to other countries or other cities than Palestine or Jerusalem, and the reason therefor is to be found in the special favor with which the people looked upon the Holy Land and the Holy City. They were considered the places set apart for the Hebrews, where they could reside under the special protection of the Deity.

[1] At the Roman Law the period of limitation was five years, and if the husband was taken captive and did not return within this period, his wife could marry again without first sending him a Bill of Divorce. (Digest, Book xlix, Title xv, Fragment xii, Section iv.)

[2] Talmud Babli Kethuboth 110 b.

"It is better to live in Palestine," says an anonymous Talmudical authority, "even in a city where the majority are Gentiles, than to live outside of Palestine, even in a city where the majority are Jews; for one dwelling outside of the land of Canaan is to be considered as though he had no God, as it is written,[1] 'I am the Lord your God which brought you forth out of the land of Egypt *to give you the land of Canaan and to be your God*,' and as it is furthermore written[2] that David said, when he fled before Saul, 'They have driven me out this day from abiding in the inheritance of the Lord saying, Go serve other gods.'"[3] Residence in Palestine was closely associated with the protection of Divine Providence, and one dwelling in a foreign country was in a sense removed from such protection.

Another element which led to this assignment of superiority to Palestine was the natural and deep-rooted affection which it, and particularly the City of Jerusalem, had awakened in the popular mind, after the return from the Babylonian captivity. It was then that the patriotism and loyalty of the people to their mother country, raised it to be the dwelling place *par excellence* of the Jew, and established the right of the wife to refuse to follow her husband in case he desired to remove her beyond its boundaries.

Under the later law the principle was extended.

[1] Leviticus xxv, 38.
[2] 1 Samuel xxvi, 19
[3] Talmud Babli Kethuboth 110 b.

If a man was about to leave the jurisdiction of the court, no matter in what country, to go to another country, he was either placed under oath not to desert his wife, or, if he insisted on going, was compelled to divorce her.[1]

APOSTASY.—An Israelite who apostatized was not *ipso facto* divorced from his wife; his contract of marriage was binding,[2] and his wife, therefore, could be divorced only by a Get in the usual form.[3] The solidarity of the Jews still kept the apostate within the brotherhood in spite of his transgression;[4] but his apostasy was deemed a sufficient ground for divorce.

As the Jewish courts, however, in such cases had lost their authority over him, it was deemed lawful to appeal to the Gentile Courts presided over by judges who were of his new faith,[5] to carry out the mandate of the Jewish Courts of Law. This proceeding was resorted to during the Middle Ages, and precedents for it were found in the early Talmudical times, when appeals were had to the Heathen courts to carry the Jewish order of divorce into execution.[6]

HUSBAND'S LICENTIOUSNESS.—As long as po-

[1] Eben Haëzer cliv, 8-9
[2] Talmud Babli Kethuboth 30 b.
[3] Maimonides' Treatise Ishuth iv, 15.
[4] At Roman Law loss of citizenship, which was equivalent to dissolution of religious community, did not dissolve the marriage unless the innocent party consented thereto (Code of Justinian, Book v, Title xvii, Const. i).
[5] Beth Joseph 134.
[6] Mishnah Gittin ix, 8.

lygamy and concubinage were legally sanctioned, there was a very marked distinction made between the sexual immorality of the husband and that of the wife. Adultery, technically speaking, could be committed only by the wife; and the married man who had formed connections with other women was not guilty of that offense in the same sense. After polygamy and concubinage had been interdicted by custom, the licentious conduct of the husband was deemed more serious in the eye of the law, and if he persisted in it, by associating with harlots or other depraved persons, his wife was entitled to be divorced from him.[1] Polygamy was lawful, but not generally countenanced, and Rabbi Ami (about 300 C.E.) went to the length of saying that a man had no legal right to marry a second wife without the consent of his first wife, and that the latter was entitled to a divorce from him, if he did not first consult her; but this opinion did not prevail against the old law, that a man may marry as many wives as he can support.[2] The legal right to marry more than one wife was, however, rarely exercised, many communities living in absolute monogamy even during the period of the Mishnah,[3] long before the decree of Rabbi Ger-

[1] Rabbi Isserles to Eben Haëzer cliv, 1.
[2] Talmud Babli Yebamoth 65 a.
[3] There are many indications in the Mishnah that monogamy was the rule and polygamy the exception. In Mishnah Yebamoth ii, 9 and 10, it is stated that, among others, the messenger who brings the Get from foreign parts shall not marry the divorced woman; but if the messenger was a married man at the time when he brought the Get and his wife after-

shom (about 1025 C.E.), by which polygamy was officially interdicted.

DIVORCE OF BETROTHED WIFE.—The betrothal, anciently, took place twelve months before the marriage, the bride meanwhile remaining with her parents, but being in all other respects bound as a wife, and freed only by death or divorce; hence, the various laws respecting the right of the woman to a divorce apply as well to the betrothed as to the married woman.[1]

wards died, he was then permitted to marry the divorced woman. The presumption that he had assisted in divorcing her because he wished to marry her himself, is rebutted by the fact that he had a wife living at the time. See infra, p. 108.

[1] Mishnah Kethuboth v, 2. In the case of Lindo *vs.* Belisario, 1. Hagg. Consist. Repts. 216 (1795), Lord Stowell in a long and learned opinion discusses the Jewish Law of betrothal and marriage, and points out the essential distinction between them. The case is interesting on account of the large number of experts in the Jewish Law who were called to testify, and whose opinions are cited at length.

CHAPTER VII.

RECONCILIATION AND REMARRIAGE.

Attempt to Reconcile the Couple a Duty of the Rabbis Under the Law—Rabbi was Legal and Spiritual Adviser—Absolving Husband from Vow to Divorce his Wife—Remarriage of Divorced Couple—Prohibition of the Remarriage of the Divorced Couple after the Wife had been Married to Another—The Deuteronomic Law—Views of Philo and Jesus Mohammedan Law—The Issue of such Unlawful Marriage is nevertheless Legitimate—Other Persons whom the Divorced Wife may not Marry.

WHILE conceding the right of the husband to divorce his wife, and the right of the wife to sue for divorce from her husband, the law nevertheless sought to prevent divorce without cause by every means within its power, short of an absolute denial of the legal right. The close union between matters spiritual and temporal among the Jews made "The Law" not merely the rule of action regulating the conduct of men in the ordinary transactions of life, but included in this term the ethical standards and religious ideals of the people. The Rabbi was judge, legal adviser, spiritual guide and religious instructor. This combination of functions resulted in establishing a system of equitable rules among the Jews separate and apart from the Law. These equitable rules and maxims were merely hortatory, and represented the moral principle protesting against an inequitable application of purely legal rules. But as these equitable principles were expounded by the same Rabbis who laid down the law, they received the acknowledgment of the people and came in time to have almost the same force and effect as the law itself; so that in the Codes of Law will be found legal rules and equitable maxims and admonitions side by side.

The reconciliation of persons about to be divorced, or who had already been divorced, afforded a fair field for the application of these ethical precepts. Besides the legal safeguards against unreasonable and ill-advised divorces, moral suasion was a potent factor,[1] and it was the duty of the judges or Rabbis to exercise their influence in checking the unrestrained passions that often prompted men to divorce their wives without cause.

If a man vowed or took an oath to divorce his wife, he was obliged, in accordance with the Mosaic Law, to fulfil his vow: "If a man make a vow unto the Lord, or swear an oath to bind his soul with an obligation, he shall not profane his word, according to all that proceeded out of his mouth shall he do."[2] To take an oath to do a certain thing, and not to perform the obligation was deemed sacrilege

---

[1] According to an old tradition the greatest glory of Aaron the High Priest was his work in reconciling discontented husbands and wives and inducing them to live together in harmony.—Aboth di Rabbi Nathan 12.

[2] Numbers xxx, 3.

"Ye shall not swear by my name falsely;"[1] and the person thus offending was punished by the infliction of thirty-nine stripes.[2] But it was always possible for a man to annul his vow by retracting and assigning as a reason rashness, heedlessness or mistake, and having his retraction confirmed in the presence of the court, whose duty it was to pronounce him free from his obligation.

When a man vowed to divorce his wife and went to the Beth Din (Court) for the purpose of having the Bill of Divorce prepared, it was the duty of the judges to use their utmost endeavor to dissuade him from carrying out his purpose, by pointing out to him all of the evil consequences of such an act; if after such an appeal by the judges, the husband expressed his regret for having intended to divorce his wife, they could at once absolve him from his vow.[3] The judges appealed to his sense of honor and self-respect, and they pleaded with him in behalf of the good name of his children. They said to him, "Do you know that to-morrow people will say of you, This man is accustomed to divorce his wives. And your daughters will become objects of scorn and will be pointed out as the daughters of the divorced woman, and people will assume that you divorced your wife because of some guilty conduct on her part, and the disgrace will fall on your children." If, after such an appeal, the husband admitted that if he had known

[1] Leviticus xix. 12; Exodus xx, 7.
[2] Mishnah Shebuoth iii, 4.
[3] Mishnah Nedarim ix, 9.

all of this he would not have vowed to divorce his wife, the court seized upon this expression of regret on his part to absolve him from his vow.[1]

After the parties had been divorced, the law favored a remarriage. The School of Shammai held that if a man had divorced his wife, and remained with her at an inn, she required no second Get;[2] *i. e.*, there was no presumption of remarriage; but the School of Hillel were of the opposite opinion, which prevailed, holding this to be a sufficient indication of an intention to live together again as man and wife.[3]

After the remarriage had taken place, the old Get by which the woman was divorced lost all validity and force, and if, for any reason, another divorce was contemplated, a new Get was required.[4]

If the Get was lost, and some one found it, he was not obliged to return it, for it was presumed that after it was written the husband changed his mind and threw it away,[5] and this presumption warranted the finder in not returning it to its owner.

The remarriage of a divorced couple was permitted during the Middle Days of Passover and the Feast of Tabernacles,[6] although new marriages

[1] Mishnah Nedarim ix, 9.
[2] Mishnah Eduyoth iv, 7.
[3] Ibid.
[4] Ibid.
[5] Mishnah Baba Meçia i, 7.
[6] Mishnah Moëd Qaton iii, 3; if the couple had been divorced after betrothal but before the marriage had been consummated, the reconciliation was deemed a new marriage and was not permitted during the festive season.—Talmud Yerushalmi Moëd Qaton i, 7 (80 d).

were forbidden during these days. The reconciliation was a continuation of the marriage formerly existing between the divorced couple and was not deemed a new marriage. Hence the provision "when a man has taken a new wife he shall not go out to war,"[1] was held not to apply to the case of a man who had remarried his divorced wife, and such a one was not exempt from military service.[2]

PROHIBITION OF THE REMARRIAGE OF THE DIVORCED COUPLE AFTER THE WIFE HAD BEEN MARRIED TO ANOTHER.—In the pre Deuteronomic age, the divorced woman who had gone to be married to another man, and who had been freed from the second marriage, could again be married to her first husband. In the Deuteronomic Code this was expressly forbidden. Remarriage with the divorced wife offended the moral sense of the Hebrews, who looked upon it as an "abomination before the Eternal."[3] This strong condemnation of what was, no doubt, established custom, cannot fail to arrest attention. The prophet Jeremiah alluding to this law calls the remarriage a "pollution." "They say if a man put away his wife, and she go from him, and become another man's, shall he return to her again? Shall not that land be greatly polluted?"[4]

There is here a curious blending of the purely

---

[1] Deuteronomy xxiv, 5.
[2] Mishnah Sotah viii, 3.
[3] Deuteronomy xxiv, 4. Abominations in the Deuteronomic sense are crimes such as idolatry, witchcraft, offences against the Levitical laws, false weights and measures, etc.
[4] Jeremiah iii, 1.

legal and the ethical view of the matter. The divorced woman was not forbidden to contract a second marriage; but, having done so, she was thereby forever deprived of the right to remarry the first husband who had divorced her. She had become "defiled" for him. The law intimates that even after her divorce, the wife had still clinging unto her some of the duties of wifehood; for the marriage of the divorced woman, although entirely legal, was deemed improper, a *quasi*-adultery.[1] There seems to have been some analogy between the case of the divorced woman who had married another and the case of the adulteress; and even as the law would not permit a man to live with an adulterous wife, so he was forbidden to live in a second marriage with his divorced wife, if she had in the meantime been the wife of another. Adultery was punished by death,[2] and if the analogy between the two cases is a true one, the offence of remarriage with the divorced woman should also be punished by death. On this point Deuteronomy is silent. Philo, in commenting on the law, uses the following strong language:[3] "But if any man should choose to form an alliance with such a woman, he must be content to bear the reputation of effeminacy . . . and as having stamped on his character two of the greatest iniquities, adultery and the employment

[1] Commentaries of Aben Ezra and Naḥmanides to Deuteronomy xxiv, 4.
[2] Deuteronomy xxii, 22; Leviticus xx, 10.
[3] "Of Special Laws against Adultery," etc , Chap. v, Yonge's Edition, Vol. III, p. 311.

of a pander; for the reconciliations which take place subsequently, are indications of the death of each; let him therefore suffer the punishment appointed together with his wife." This was the opinion of the great Jewish moralist of Alexandria.[1]

Jesus, the great Palestinian moralist, was equally severe in his condemnation. According to his view the marriage of the divorced woman to another man was adultery. "Whosoever marrieth her that is put away committeth adultery."[2] Paul likewise condemns it, saying, "Let not the wife depart from her husband, but if she depart, let her remain unmarried or be reconciled to her husband."[3]

The death penalty was rarely inflicted at Jewish law for adultery[4] or any other crime, and was practically abolished forty years before the destruction of the Temple.[5] It is not mentioned in the Talmud to have ever been inflicted in the case of a remarriage with a divorced wife after she had been married to another. The parties to such an unlawful marriage were forced to separate.[6]

By a curious perversity, Mohammed declared the very opposite of the law in Deuteronomy to be the proper rule for his people. "You may divorce your wives twice; and then either retain them

---

[1] 10 B. C. E. to 60 C. E.
[2] Luke xvi, 18; Matthew xix, 9.
[3] 1 Corinthians vii, 10–11.
[4] Talmud Babli Gittin 17 b.
[5] Talmud Babli Makkoth 7 a; Id. Sanhedrin 41 a.
[6] Mishnah Derekh Ereç 1; Mishnah Yebamoth iv, 2.

with humanity or dismiss them with kindness."[1] Until the third divorce the husband "had more right to her than any one else had" and she could not be married to another until after the third divorce. "But if the husband divorce her a third time she shall not be lawful for him again, until she marry another husband. But if he also divorce her, it shall be no crime in them if they return to each other."[2]

The moral reason for the Deuteronomic law evidently did not appeal to Mohammed. And it seems to have been obscured also in the minds of the Rabbis by the technical sense of the law, for they held that although the woman could not be remarried to her first husband after her second marriage, yet if she had been divorced and then lived in illicit relation with another man, her husband could remarry her, *for she had not been married to another.*[3]

The marriage thus declared unlawful having been dissolved by the court, the question arose as to the legitimacy of the issue of such union. Rabbi Aqiba decided that the child was a bastard, but the sages overruled him, holding that the offence of the parents was not to be visited upon their offspring, and relying on the law in Deuteronomy, which they construed thus:—the woman in such case is declared to be "an abomination," and upon the principle that "the naming of the one is the

[1] Koran Sûra 2.
[2] Ibid.
[3] Mishnah Sotah ii, 6; Eben Haëzer x, 1.

exclusion of the other," the child is not to be considered an abomination, *i. e.*, illegitimate.¹

OTHER CASES OF PROHIBITION OF REMARRIAGE.—Five other cases are cited in the Mishnah in which the husband cannot marry his wife again after he has divorced her. All of them, however, seem to have been merely recommendations, suggesting the proper conduct of the parties under the circumstances, but not having the force of law. For, if the husband, in spite of the prohibition, remarried his divorced wife, the marriage was valid and lawful.

First.—Where the woman had been divorced by her husband upon suspicion of her adultery, which had risen through an "evil report" about her.²

Second.—Where the husband divorced his wife because she had subjected herself to the obligation of vows.³

Rabbi Meïr stated that this law was intended to prevent the nullification of the Get by the husband in case he regretted the divorce. For after having been divorced the woman could be married to another man; her former husband having learned that the vow on account of which he divorced her could have been annulled by him, might express his regret at the divorce saying, If I had known this I would not have divorced her if you had given me a hundred talents (of silver). This would have

---
¹ Mishnah Yebamoth iv, 12; Talmud Babli Yebamoth 44 b.
² Mishnah Gittin iv, 7.
³ Ibid.

sufficed to annul the Get, invalidate the second marriage and bastardize her issue by her second husband.

Rabbi Elazar (about 100 C.E.) was of the opinion that the reason for this law was to warn the women to be careful and circumspect in their conduct so as not to give occasion for any suspicion, and not to be reckless in making vows.[1]

Third.—Where the husband has divorced his wife because she is barren.[2]

Fourth.—Where a third person has guaranteed the payment of the Kethubah to the wife.

The husband cannot remarry her after he had divorced her, because it is possible that he might divorce her in order that she may claim her Kethubah from the guarantor, and then by marrying her again he would enjoy the benefit of the Kethubah which she had collected. Rabbi Simon ben Gamañel thought it possible that such a scheme to defraud might arise, and therefore recommended that remarriage in such cases be prohibited.[3]

Fifth.—Where one has consecrated all of his property to religious uses, subject to the wife's Kethubah, he must, according to Rabbi Elazar, on divorcing her, renounce his right to remarry her, lest the divorce and remarriage be used as a scheme to re-possess himself of his property through her, as in the fourth case above mentioned. For when she is divorced she is entitled

[1] Talmud Babli Gittin 46 a.
[2] Mishnah Gittin iv, 11.
[3] Mishnah Baba Bathra x, 9.

to claim her Kethubah and take the property which has been dedicated by her husband to religious uses; and after having obtained it she might re-marry her husband and thus place him again in possession of his property. But Rabbi Joshua was of the opinion that a man is not to be presumed to have sinister designs on sacred things, and that if he has consecrated his property to religious uses, he will not use such pretext to regain possession of it.[1]

[1] Mishnah Erakhin vi, 2.

CHAPTER VIII.

JUDICIAL SEPARATIONS UNDER THE QUASI-CRIMINAL
JURISDICTION OF THE RABBIS.

Incest—Marriage of Hebrew and Heathen—The Great Reform of Ezra –Mamzer—Nethin Adulteress and Paramour—The Ordeal of the Bitter Waters—Lepers—Forbidden Marriages of the Priests—Re-marriage of the Divorced Couple after the Wife had been Married to Another—Yebama—Childless Marriages.

ALTHOUGH not strictly cases of divorce, judicial separations by the court in the exercise of a quasi-criminal jurisdiction, must be noticed here. In these cases the marriage was declared void, on grounds of public policy; no Bill of Divorce was required, as no legal marriage existed. In some instances such judicial separations were followed by the infliction of the death penalty on the guilty couple, in others by the thirty-nine stripes with the lash.

INCEST.—The sexual crimes enumerated in the eighteenth chapter of Leviticus are included in this class of cases.[1]

MARRIAGE OF A HEBREW AND A HEATHEN.—The Torah[2] mentions seven heathen nations with whom marriage was forbidden. The Rabbis forbade mar-

[1] Maimonides' Treatise Issuré Biah i, 4-7.
[2] Deuteronomy vii, 1-3.

riage with all non-Jewish people.[1] The reason for the Biblical prohibition of intermarriage was the fear lest idolatry should be introduced into Israel; and this reason applied with equal force to all heathen nations as well as to the seven nations especially mentioned. This was the interpretation of Ezra[2] when he ordained that all the Hebrews who had returned from the exile must put away their heathen wives.

The great religious gain of the people on their return from Babylonian captivity was the reaction from polytheism. A necessary sequence to this monotheistic revival was the abhorrence of marriage with the heathen. This was at first characteristic of certain zealous members of the priestly class, but within a short time it gained almost universal acceptance among the people, and has remained one of the distinguishing peculiarities of the Jewish race until this day. The people had been told by their teachers and prophets that their sufferings were the result of their own transgression and of their intimate intercourse with the lascivious heathen nations, and that a complete severance of all intercourse with the source of this infection was their only salvation. That was the reason of the sweeping reforms of Ezra and Nehemiah and of the denunciations of the prophet Malachi (about 450 B.C.).

In the memoirs of Ezra, this great reform is described in simple yet dramatic words:

[1] Talmud Babli Abodah Zarah 36 b.
[2] Ezra, chap. viii–x passim.

"Now when these things were done the princes approached me, saying, The people of Israel, and the priests, and the Levites, have not separated themselves from the people of the lands. . . . For they have taken of their daughters for themselves, and for their sons. . . . And when I heard this thing, I rent my garment and my mantle, and plucked out some of the hair of my head and of my beard, and sat down astounded . . . and I sat astounded until the evening sacrifice. And at the evening sacrifice I arose up from my fasting, and with my rent garment and mantle, I fell upon my knees and spread out my hands unto the Lord my God."

While Ezra was praying the people gathered and stood around in tearful silence, and finally one of them rose and said,

"We have trespassed against our God, and have taken strange wives of the people of the land; yet now there is hope in Israel concerning this thing. Now, therefore, let us make a covenant with our God to put away all the wives, and such as are born of them . . . *and let it be done according to the law.* . . . Then arose Ezra and made the chief priests, the Levites and all Israel, to swear that they should do according to this word. And they sware."

Three days thereafter, a great convocation was held in Jerusalem, and the people sat in the open place in the Temple Court, "trembling because of this matter, and for the great rain," and Ezra addressed them saying, "Ye have transgressed, and have taken strange wives, to increase the trespass of Israel. Now, therefore, make confession unto the Lord God of your fathers, and do his pleasure; and separate yourselves from the people of the land, and from the strange wives. Then all the congregation answered and said with a loud voice, As thou hast said so must we do." [1]

Nehemiah, in his memoirs, also refers to this event, and expresses no uncertain opinion about those who had taken strange wives. His account begins as follows: "On that day they read in the Book of Moses in the audience of the people; and therein was found written that the Ammonite and the Moabite should not come into the congregation of God forever.[2] . . . . Now it came to pass, when they had heard the law, that they separated from Israel all the alien mixture."[3]

The wall of separation thus raised between Jews and non-Jews did not at first exclude Christians. The latter were merely a Jewish sect; and it was not until the doctrine of the Trinity was established among them, that the Rabbinical interdict was applied to them. Shortly after the Roman Empire became Christian officially, an imperial decree declared the marriage of Jew and Christian unlawful and the parties guilty of the "crime of adultery."[4] This law served to strengthen the barriers between Jew and Christian; it was copied by all the mediæval lawmakers and enforced with much holy zeal.

[1] Ezra, chaps. ix-x passim.
[2] Deuteronomy xxiii, 3-4.
[3] Nehemiah xiii, 1-3.
[4] Code of Justinian, Book i, Title ix, Sec. v.

JUDICIAL SEPARATIONS.

MARRIAGE WITH A MAMZER OR A NETHIN.—The Hebrews were prohibited from marrying a mamzer or a nethin; the law applying equally to males and females.[1]

The Mamzer was one born of an adulterous, incestuous or other unlawful connection,[2] and was not permitted to enter "the Congregation of the Lord."[3]

The *Nethinim* were supposed to be the descendants of the Gibeonites;[4] but this will hardly account for the degraded position they occupied. Mr. Joseph Jacobs[5] has suggested a far more probable meaning of the term. He identifies them with the descendants of the sacred prostitutes who haunted the Temple during the reign of the kings who imported the idolatries of the surrounding nations into Israel.

THE ADULTERESS.—Under the Mosaic Law both the adulteress and *particeps criminis* were put to death,[6] only, however, when taken in the crime.[7] When the woman was suspected of the crime, she was obliged to submit to the ordeal of drinking the "bitter waters," and was charged with a most solemn oath, which was calculated to reassure her if she was innocent and to elicit a confession from her if she was guilty.[8]

[1] Mishnah Yebamoth viii, 3.
[2] Ibid. iv, 13.
[3] Deuteronomy xxiii, 3.
[4] Joshua ix, passim; 2 Samuel xxi, 2-6.
[5] Biblical Archæology, p. 104, *et seq*.
[6] Leviticus xx, 10; xviii, 20.
[7] Deuteronomy xxii, 22.
[8] Mishnah Sotah i, 1.

THE ORDEAL OF THE BITTER WATERS.—"If any man's wife go aside and commit a trespass against him, and a man lie with her carnally, and it be hidden from the eyes of her husband, because she has been secretly defiled, and there be no witness against her, and she be not detected in the fact; and the spirit of jealousy come upon him, and he be jealous of his wife, and she have been defiled; or if the spirit of jealousy come upon him, and he be jealous of his wife, and she have not been defiled; then shall the man bring his wife unto the priest, and he shall bring her offering for her, the tenth part of an epha of barley meal; he shall not pour any oil upon it, nor put frankincense thereon; for it is an offering of jealousy, an offering of memorial, bringing iniquity to remembrance. And the priest shall bring her near, and place her before the Lord; and the priest shall take holy water in an earthen vessel; and of the dust that is in the floor of the tabernacle the priest shall take, and put it into the water; and the priest shall place the woman before the Lord, and uncover the woman's head, and put in her hands the offering of memorial, which is the jealousy offering; and in the hand of the priest shall be the bitter waters that bring the curse; and the priest shall charge her by an oath, and say unto the woman, If no man have lain with thee, and if thou hast not gone aside to uncleanness behind thy husband, be thou free from these bitter waters that bring the curse; but if thou hast gone aside behind thy husband, and if thou hast been defiled, and some man have lain with thee besides thine husband—then the priest shall charge the woman with an oath of cursing, and the priest shall say unto the woman—The Lord make thee a curse and an oath among thy people, when the Lord doth cause thy thigh to fall away, and thy belly to swell; and these waters that bring the curse shall go into thy bowels, to cause the belly to swell and the thigh to fall away. And the woman shall say, Amen, Amen. And the priest shall write these curses on a roll, and he shall blot them out with the bitter waters; and he shall cause the woman to drink the bitter waters that bring the curse, and the waters that bring the curse shall enter into her for bitterness. Then the priest shall take the jealousy offering out of the woman's hand, and shall wave the offering before the Lord, and bring it near to the altar; and the priest shall take a handful of the offering, as a memorial thereof, and burn it upon the altar, and afterward shall cause the woman to drink the water. And when he hath made her drink the water, then it shall come to pass, that if she have been defiled, and have committed trespass against her husband, that the waters that bring the curse shall enter into her for bitterness, and her belly shall swell, and her thigh shall fall away; and the woman shall be a curse among her people. And if the woman have not been defiled, but be clean, then she shall remain unharmed and shall conceive seed."

"This is the law of jealousies, when a wife goeth aside behind her husband and hath been defiled; or when the spirit of jealousy cometh upon him, and he be jealous of his wife, and he shall place the woman before the Lord, and the priest shall do unto her according to all this law. And the man shall be guiltless from iniquity, and this woman shall bear her iniquity."[1]

CONFESSION OF GUILT.—If the woman under the stress of the ordeal confessed her crime, she was obliged to separate at once from her husband.[2] The oath administered by the officiating priest was calculated to inspire a guilty woman with terror, and the innocent woman was reassured by the words, "If no man have lain with thee, and if thou hast not gone aside to uncleanness behind thy husband, be thou free from these bitter waters that bring the curse." If, however, the woman refused to submit to the ordeal, and there was circumstantial evidence of criminality, she was declared guilty, and a separation was decreed as if her guilt had been fully proven.[3]

The adultery of the wife having been proven, there could be no condonation by the husband;[4] this was against the spirit of Jewish law.

The Biblical law of capital punishment for adultery was abolished at an early period, and thereafter the judicial decree of separation was rigidly enforced; the woman lost her Kethubah,[5] and was not permitted to marry her paramour.[6]

[1] Numbers v, 12–31.
[2] Mishnah Sotah i, 5.
[3] Id. iii, 6; iv, 2.
[4] Id. v, 1; Mishnah Yebamoth x, 1.
[5] Maimonides' Ishuth, xxiv, 6.
[6] Mishnah Sotah v, 1; Mishnah Yebamoth ii, 8.

ABOLITION OF THE ORDEAL OF THE "BITTER WATERS."—Whatever may have been the significance of this ordeal when first established, it came within Talmudic times to have merely a moral meaning. It was simply a test under which the woman, if guilty, was likely to succumb and confess. The Rabbis said, "only when the man is himself free from guilt will the waters be an effective test of the wife's guilt or innocence; and if he has been guilty of illicit intercourse the waters will be of none effect."[1] During the military invasion of Palestine, and in the last days of the Jewish Commonwealth, the Sanhedrin under Rabbi Yohanan ben Zakkai abolished the ordeal entirely.[2]

LEPERS.—Under the Mosaic law a person afflicted with leprosy was excluded from the society of men, and was obliged to live "outside the camp;" "his garments shall be rent, and his head shall be bare, and he shall cover himself up to his lip and Unclean, unclean, he shall call out."[3] In chapter xii of Leviticus there is an elaborate series of tests prescribed in diagnosing this disease.

If the disease attacks husband or wife, the Court will immediately decree a separation of the parties,[4] even though they desire to continue the marriage relation.[5] Where, however, they agree not to live

[1] Talmud Babli Sotah 47 b.
[2] Mishnah Sotah ix, 9.
[3] Leviticus xiii, 45–46.
[4] Talmud Babli Kethuboth 77 b.
[5] Ibid.

closeted together provided their marriage is not annulled, the Courts will not interfere.[1]

KOHANIM.—The Kohanim[2] or members of the priestly tribe of Aaron were forbidden to marry a divorced woman, a harlot or a Hallalah,[3] *i. e.*, one born of the union of a priest and a woman whom he was forbidden to marry. The High-priest was also forbidden to marry a widow. The reason for these prohibitions was obviously to preserve a high standard of domestic purity in the priestly families. But even after the temple was destroyed the injunction against these marriages was not thereby dissolved, and it is binding to this day on many Jews who claim descent from Aaron. Under the Talmudic law the woman who had become a Haluçah[4] was also forbidden to the priest, she being considered a divorced woman.[5]

REMARRIAGE WITH DIVORCED WIFE.—The remarriage of the husband to his divorced wife after she had been married to another was forbidden by a positive law of the Bible;[6] such an act was deemed a flagrant immorality.

YEBAMA.—A Yebama[7] could not marry a stranger before she had been renounced by her brother-in-law, whose betrothed she became at the death of her husband.[8]

[1] Talmud Babli Kethuboth 77 b.
[2] Leviticus xxi, 7.
[3] Ibid. 14.
[4] Deuteronomy xxv, 4-10.
[5] Talmud Babli Yebamoth 24 a.
[6] Deuteronomy xxiv, 1-4.
[7] Id. xxv, 4 10.
[8] Infra, page 170.

CHILDLESS MARRIAGES.—The Hebrews deemed marriage a failure unless it resulted in the birth of issue; a large family was especially desirable,[1] and sterility was considered a curse.[2] A Boraitha states that if a couple have lived together for ten years and no children are born to them, the husband ought to give his wife a Bill of Divorce, for the object of marriage has been defeated,[3] and Mar Samuel held that the Court will compel him to divorce her.[4] His opinion prevailed, although this practice soon fell into abeyance.[5] The Rabbis continued to urge divorce in such cases, but did not compel the couple to separate if they preferred to dwell together as man and wife in spite of the childlessness of their union. The Rabbis used moral suasion in such cases rather than force; they urged men and women to subordinate their natural passions to a higher principle, and taught that a marriage without issue was unholy. If, however, the parties did not wish to separate, the husband was encouraged to take another wife, in addition to his first wife, so that the object of marriage, the birth of children, should be attained. Philo's opinion on this question reflects the current Rabbinical view. Although he considered persons who had no children, and who nevertheless would not separate, as worthy of pardon because they

[1] Talmud Babli Yebamoth 61 b, 62 a.
[2] Deuteronomy vii, 14.
[3] Talmud Babli Yebamoth 64 a.
[4] Talmud Babli Kethuboth 77 a.
[5] Rabbi Isserles to Eben Haëzer i, 3; cliv, 10.

were influenced by habit and familiarity, motives of great weight, yet he recommended divorce in such cases, lest the gratification of the senses be considered more desirable than progeny.[1]

[1] Philo, "On Special Laws, etc.," vi, Yonge's Edition, Vol. III, p. 312.

CHAPTER IX.

THE LEGAL AND SOCIAL STATUS OF THE DIVORCED WOMAN.

Divorced Woman is *Sui Juris*—Cannot Marry a Kohen (Priest)—Under the Old Law no Odium Attached to the Divorced Woman—Change Under Later Law—Divorced Woman Liable for her Torts—Bound by Her Vows—She may Give Herself in Marriage to Anyone—If Suspected of Adultery she Cannot Marry her Paramour—Nor the Messenger Bringing her Bill of Divorce—Nor the Rabbi who Refuses to Absolve her Vows—She must not Marry within Three Months after her Divorce.

The legal and social status of the divorced woman is but vaguely touched upon in the Bible. There is nothing to indicate that her position was in any sense an inferior one; but, on the contrary, she seems to have enjoyed certain advantages denied to married women. The divorced woman, like the widow, was *sui juris*. Before her marriage the woman was subject to the authority of her father (*patria potestas*); during the marriage her husband was her master; if widowed or divorced, she did not again become subject to her father's *potestas*, but became her own mistress. She then had the right to give herself in marriage,[1] whereas

[1] Deuteronomy xxiv, 2.

(101)

as a maiden, before her maturity, she was given in marriage by her father; and unlike an unmarried woman or a wife, she could bind herself by her vows.[1] The only absolute disadvantage that a bill of divorce wrought for the woman was the denial of her right to marry a Kohen, or Priest. "They shall not take a harlot or one that is profaned, neither a woman that is put away from her husband shall they (the priests) take; for he is holy unto his God."[2] The divorced woman is here classed in bad society, and the widow seems to be favored by the law, inasmuch as she was permitted to be married to a priest. It is, however, quite natural to look more favorably upon a woman who is freed from the bond of matrimony by the death of her husband than upon one who has been divorced, and whose husband is perhaps still living. If it be borne in mind that in theory the divorced woman still had some of the duties of wifehood clinging to her, it will be understood why the priest, who must be free from all defilement, was forbidden to take such a woman as his wife. Philo says: "They (the priests) are permitted with impunity to marry not only maidens, but widows also; not indeed all widows, but those whose husbands are dead, for the law thinks it fitting to remove all quarrels and disputes from the life of the priest; and if they have husbands living, there very likely might be disputes from the jealousy which is caused by the love of men for women; but when

[1] Numbers xxx, 10.
[2] Leviticus xxi, 7.

the first husband is dead, then with him the hostility which could be felt towards the second husband dies also."[1]

The High Priest, by virtue of his exalted and sanctified station, was not permitted to marry a woman other than a virgin. "A widow or a divorced woman or one profaned or a harlot, these shall he (the High Priest) not take, but a virgin of his own people shall he take for wife."[2] Here the widow is in the same class with the divorced woman, and the less respectable members of society.

The marriage with the divorced woman seems, therefore, to have been simply a mesalliance for a priest, and there was no other odium attached to her position. Her ineligibility for marriage with a priest did not extend to her daughter, the latter being in no way affected by the status of her mother.[3] In the days of Ezekiel, after the Babylonian captivity, the Priests and the Levites, the sons of Zadok,[4] were commanded "not to take for their wives a widow, nor her that is put away,"[5] exception being made in favor of the widow of the priest. Here, then, all distinction between the widow and the divorced woman disappears. The last proof that the divorced woman was in no sense under the sentence of social or religious ostracism,

[1] Philo, "On Monarchy," Book ii, Chap. x, Yonge's Edition, Vol. III, p. 199.
[2] Leviticus xxi, 14.
[3] Mishnah Derekh Ereç i.
[4] Ezekiel xliv, 15.
[5] Ibid. 22.

is furnished by the Law of the Priest's Daughter.[1] "And if the daughter of a priest be married unto a stranger, she may not eat of the offered part of holy things, but the daughter of a priest, if she be a widow or divorced, and have no children, and is returned unto her father's house as in her youth, may eat of her father's bread; but no stranger shall eat thereof." Here the daughter of the priest during her marriage, while in the *manus* of her husband, partakes of his religious status, and if he be a stranger, that is to say, not a priest, she loses the right that she had in her father's house to eat of the offerings. But after she has been freed by the death of her husband, or has been divorced from him, she may return to her father's house and be reinvested with her former right to eat of the offered part of holy things.

As divorce was the right of the husband, to be exercised by him at his pleasure, no disgrace could attach to the status of a divorced woman, because she might have been sent away by her husband at any time for no reason whatsoever; but when in the course of time this right of the husband was restricted, and he was obliged to show cause before his divorce received Rabbinical sanction, the status of the divorced woman underwent a corresponding change. During the Talmudic period divorces without cause seem to have become rare, and women who had been sent away by their husbands were looked upon with suspicion. Unless the woman could show that the divorce had been

---

[1] Leviticus zxii, 12-13.

granted at her request, or by the order of the Court on her application, she was suspected of having been guilty of some offence which prompted her husband to send her away.[1] This sentiment grew so strong that it was considered disgraceful to marry a divorced woman,[2] who was *prima facie* "a wicked woman" who had been turned out of her first husband's house because of her shameful conduct.

Corresponding to this change in the status of the divorced woman, was the change in the nature of divorce proceedings. The husband's ancient right to divorce at his pleasure, was restricted by law and morals, and nearly all divorces were *coram judice*. In most cases when the cause for which the divorce was sought was trifling, the influence of the Rabbis, or of mutual friends and relatives, was sufficient to reconcile the parties and prevent the divorce, and the majority of divorces were given only where adequate cause existed.

THE DIVORCED WOMAN IS *sui juris*.—As was shown above, the references in the Torah to the legal and social status of the divorced woman are meagre, but there is enough to indicate that she was entirely *sui juris*, being no longer under the power of her husband nor, in a legal sense, a member of the household of her father. The Mishnah says that the woman "comes into her own power" (obtains her freedom) by a bill of divorce or by the death of her husband,[3] whereby

[1] Mishnah Nedarim ix, 9.
[2] Talmud Babli Gittin 90 b.
[3] Mishnah Qiddushin i, 1.

she is invested with all the rights and liabilities of a single woman, who has been emancipated by her father. The vows made by the widow or the divorced woman were, under the Mosaic law, binding upon her,[1] whereas the vows of the married woman could be annulled by her husband. If the divorced woman re-married, the obligations which she had assumed by her vow were still binding upon her and could not be annulled by her second husband.[2]

Another illustration of the difference between the status of the married woman and that of the divorced woman was their respective liability for torts committed by them. The married woman committing a tort was not liable in damages to the person injured by her, as long as she remained married; for the property of the married woman, during her coverture, could not be attached to satisfy claims for damages against her. These claims remained a lien upon her estate, and could be enforced only when she came into possession of it after the death of her husband or upon her divorce.[3]

The divorced woman being *sui juris* could be married "to any man whom she desired."[4] One of the clauses in the Get was, "thou art permitted (to be married) to any man."[5] Her privilege, how-

---

[1] Numbers xxx, 10.
[2] Mishnah Nedarim xi, 8.
[3] Mishnah Baba Qama viii, 4.
[4] Mishnah Gittin ix, 3.
[5] Ibid.

ever, was not entirely unrestricted, her marriage to certain persons being forbidden by law.

RESTRICTIONS ON RIGHT OF DIVORCED WOMAN TO MARRY.—The divorced woman was not permitted to marry the man who was suspected of having committed adultery with her.[1] While at Roman Law she was not permitted to marry the man who had been convicted of adultery with her,[2] at Jewish law the mere suspicion of adultery was enough to prevent the marriage. A case is suggested in the Talmud in which this restriction seems to have been removed. Where the woman having been suspected of adultery was divorced, and having re-married was again divorced, and then married the person who had been suspected of having committed adultery with her, the marriage was not declared unlawful, because, it seems, the other marriage, which intervened, was looked upon as in a sense palliative of the supposed crime.[3]

The messenger bringing a Get or Bill of Divorce from foreign parts could not marry the woman who was divorced thereby.[4] Inasmuch as the validity of the divorce depended upon his testimony alone, which was accepted in lieu of the usual proof by two witnesses, there was a strong temptation for him, if he felt so inclined, to forge a Get in the absence of the husband, and by making the state-

[1] Mishnah Yebamoth ii, 8.
[2] Digest, Book xxxiv, Title ix, Fragment xiii.
[3] Talmud Yerushalmi Yebamoth sub Mishnah ii, 12 (4 b), Talmud Babli Yebamoth 24 b.
[4] Mishnah Yebamoth ii, 9.

ment that it was written and attested before him, divorce her, and then marry her himself.

Where a woman was divorced because she had made certain vows, which upon being submitted to a judge were declared binding upon her, she could not be married to him;[1] because the judge might have refused to absolve her vows to induce the husband to divorce her, in order that he (the judge) might marry her.

The reason in these cases was to prevent falsehood and self-interest from vitiating the acts of the parties; but if the circumstances were such that the reason no longer existed, the prohibition against such re-marriage was removed. So that where more than one messenger brought the Get, or a court of three judges sustained the vows of the woman, any one of the messengers or of the judges could marry her after she had been divorced.[2] And so, also, if the messenger or the judge was a married man at the time when the woman was divorced, and his wife died, he could then marry the divorced woman, as it was not to be presumed that he could have had any improper motives in the performance of his duty, or that he would have speculated upon the contingency of the death of his wife.[3]

Finally, the divorced woman was not permitted to remarry or even to be betrothed within three

---

[1] Mishnah Yebamoth ii, 10.
[2] Maimonides' Gerushin x, 16, Talmud Yerushalmi Yebamoth sub Mishnah ii, 11, 12 (4 a, b).
[3] Mishnah Yebamoth ii, 10, supra p. 76, note 3.

months after her divorce, in order that no doubt might be cast upon the paternity of the child with which she then might have been pregnant.[1]

This law was copied by Mohammed,[2] with this modification, that if the divorce was given after the betrothal but before the marriage was consummated, the woman was not obliged to wait at all before re-marrying.[3]

The Mosaic law provided that the divorced woman should not marry a priest.[4] This was not because of any stigma cast upon the woman by reason of her divorce, but because of the peculiar sanctity of the priestly office. As the law in Leviticus states that the priest shall not take a woman that is put away from her husband, it was decided that where she had been merely betrothed and then divorced, before the marriage had been consummated, a priest might marry her, and that such marriage would be entirely lawful.[5] The marriage with a divorced woman subjected the priest to the penalty of the lash, the punishment being thirty-nine stripes,[6] and a son born of such a union was not qualified to perform the usual priestly functions.[7]

[1] Mishnah Yebamoth iv, 10.
[2] Koran Sûras 2 and 65.
[3] Id. 33. The divorced wife of Mohammed was not permitted to marry; she was by a legal fiction looked upon as the mother of all the people, and therefore within the prohibition of the law forbidding incest.
[4] Leviticus xxi, 7.
[5] Mishnah Yebamoth x, 3. See also Mishnah Gittin viii, 7.
[6] Mishnah Makkoth iii, 1.
[7] Mishnah Therumoth viii, 1.

The moral law, which always sought to inculcate principles of righteousness, recommended the gentle treatment of the divorced woman, and especially praised him who supported and comforted her.[1]

It is related of Rabbi Yosé the Galilean (about 100 C. E.), that after his divorced wife had remarried and was reduced to poverty, he invited her and her husband into his house and supported them, although when she was his wife she had made his life miserable,[2] and his conduct is the subject of Rabbinical laudation.[3] "Do not withdraw from thy flesh," said Isaiah;[4] this Rabbi Jacob bar Aḥa interpreted to mean "Do not withdraw help from thy divorced wife."[5]

[1] Rabbi Isserles to Eben Haëzer cxix, 8.
[2] Talmud Yerushalmi Kethuboth sub Mishnah ,
[3] Midrash Bereshith Rabba xvii, 3.
[4] Isaiah lviii, 7.
[5] Midrash Bereshith Rabba xvii, 3.

CHAPTER X.

THE PROPERTY RIGHTS OF THE DIVORCED WOMAN
AND THE CUSTODY AND MAINTENANCE
OF HER CHILDREN.

The Kethubah—The Biblical Dowry—The Ordinance of Shimeon ben Shetaḥ—The Lien of the Kethubah—The Wife could not Waive her Rights under the Kethubah—Dowry at Mohammedan Law—The Amount of the Kethubah—Increase of the Kethubah—Payment of the Kethubah—Wife's Separate Estate—Earnings, etc., of Divorced Wife—Prescriptive Rights against her Former Husband—Cases in which the Divorced Wife lost her Kethubah by Reason of her Misconduct—Custody of Children of Divorced Woman—Nurslings—Roman Law as to Custody—Rabbinical Decisions—Support of Children at Roman Law and Jewish Law.

THE KETHUBAH.—The dowry given to the father upon the marriage of his daughter originally was the purchase money which the husband paid for her. Undeniable traces of the original commercial nature of marriage are to be found in the Bible, although the state of society which is therein described had already passed through the lower stage of matrimonial bargains. When Shehem, the son of Ḥamor, the Prince of the Hivites, desired to obtain Dinah, the daughter of Jacob, for a wife, he said unto her father and unto her brethren, " Let me find grace in your eyes and what ye

(111)

shall say unto me I will give, ask me never so much dowry and gift and I will give according as ye shall say unto me, but give me the damsel to wife."[1] Other instances are the wooing of Rebecca through Abraham's servant Eleazar, and Jacob's service with Laban for Rachel and Leah. In the case of Rebecca, the dowry sent by her future husband's father accrued to her benefit as well as that of her mother and brother;[2] whereas Jacob's service accrued solely to the benefit of Laban.[3] In the Book of Exodus we find the following: "And if a man entice a maid that is not betrothed and lie with her, he shall surely endow her to be his wife. If her father utterly refuse to give her unto him, he shall pay money according to the dowry of virgins."[4] The dowry was originally payable to the father of the wife, and late in Talmudic times this was still the law in cases where the wife was a minor or was divorced before the marriage had been consummated. Eventually, however, the dowry was given to the wife, remaining undivided in the estate of the husband, and being payable to her on her divorce, or on the death of her husband. As the heirs of the husband often defrauded the widow of her rights, it was ordained that the amount of the dowry should be deposited with the father of the wife, thus making it secure against the adverse claim of his heirs. But as it was the purpose of the institu-

[1] Genesis xxxiv, 11-12.
[2] Id. xxiv, 53.
[3] Id. xxx, 26.
[4] Exodus xxii, 15-16.

tion of the dowry to act as a check upon the husband, so that "it shall not be easy in his eyes to divorce her," the deposit of the money with the father of the wife destroyed the effect intended. As the husband had no further payment to make, there were no financial considerations to hinder him from giving the divorce whenever he pleased, and telling his wife "to go to her dowry." It was then provided by law that the amount of the dowry should be invested in articles of value, and that these should remain in possession of the husband. This regulation, however, was found to give no greater satisfaction than the former one, for it was very easy for the husband to give the articles of value to his wife and tell her to go. The final remedy, the Kethubah, was provided by an ordinance of Shimeon ben Shetaḥ.[1] He ordained that the dowry should remain with the husband and not be separated from his estate; that it should be secured to the wife by a writing,[2] whereby all his estate was charged with its payment.

THE LIEN OF THE KETHUBAH.—The Kethubah was, like the Common Law dower, a lien upon all real estate owned by the husband during his lifetime, and if after his death or when he divorced his wife he had no estate in possession, it could be collected out of the estate which he had formerly owned but which was now in the possession of third persons.[3] This regulation was a very im-

[1] Talmud Babli Shabbath 14 b. Some Talmudists consider the Kethubah a Mosaic ordinance. (Ibid.)
[2] Tobith vii, 14.
[3] Talmud Babli Kethuboth 82 b; Mishnah Gittin v, 2.

portant check upon the freedom of divorce. The wealth of the people consisted chiefly of estate in lands, and as it was necessary that the Kethubah should be paid in coin, it was often difficult for a man to obtain so large a sum, and hence gave time for reconsideration of his intention to divorce his wife.[1]

THE KETHUBAH COULD NOT BE WAIVED.—The Kethubah was an inalienable right of the wife, and marriage without a Kethubah was unlawful. Rabbi Meïr (about 150 C. E.) was of the opinion that a man was forbidden to remain with his wife even one hour, unless she had a Kethubah, "lest it appear easy to him to divorce her."[2] Even the Ravisher, who is by law prohibited from divorcing his wife, was, nevertheless, according to the opinion of Rabbi Yosé ben Juda, obliged to give her a Kethubah. The Rabbis generally were of the opinion that he need not give a Kethubah, because he could not divorce her, but Rabbi Yosé remarked that if she had no Kethubah, the husband could, by making her life miserable, compel her, in self-defence, to apply for a divorce, and thus easily get rid of her.[3] If the Kethubah was lost, a new one had to be written. The wife could not sell her Kethubah to her husband or release him from its obligation,[4] though she could sell her right to a

[1] Graetz's "Geschichte der Juden," Vol. III, p. 155 (Third Edition). The American Edition, Vol. II, p. 50, does not give the sense of the ordinance of Shimeon ben Shetah.
[2] Talmud Babli Baba Qama 87 a.
[3] Talmud Babli Kethuboth 39 b.
[4] Maimonides' Treatise Ishuth x, 10.

stranger, who would be entitled to collect the amount when she was divorced, or on the death of her husband.[1]

AT MOHAMMEDAN LAW.—Mohammed borrowed many of the provisions of the Jewish law, following it closely in many instances, and in others deliberately changing it to suit his purpose. The Koran[2] provides that "unto those who are divorced a reasonable provision is due." The faithful are commanded to "give women their dowry freely,"[3] "according to what is ordained,"[4] and, if the wife has had a larger sum allotted to her than the law requires, the husband is charged "not to take away anything therefrom,"[5] "for," asks Mohammed indignantly, "will ye take it away by slandering her, and doing her manifest injustice?"

Thus far Mohammed followed the Jewish law. In the case where a woman is divorced before her marriage has been consummated, the Koran[6] recommends the husband to pay the whole dowry to the wife, but states the law to be that she shall receive only half of what has been settled upon her.

The important departure of the Mohammedan from the Jewish law is in the right given the wife to release her dowry to her husband. At Jewish law, the wife could not waive her dower rights in

[1] Maimonides' Treatise Ishuth x, 10.
[2] Sûra 2.
[3] Ibid.
[4] Sûra 4.
[5] Ibid.
[6] Sûra 2.

favor of her husband, but at Mohammedan law this was permitted. "Give them their dowry," says the Koran,[1] "according to what is ordained, but it shall be no crime in you to make any other agreement among yourselves." "If they (the women) voluntarily remit unto you any part of it, enjoy it with satisfaction and advantage."[2]

THE AMOUNT OF THE KETHUBAH.—The amount of the dowry was two hundred zuz (or two mina) for virgins, and one-half of this amount for widows or divorced women upon their re-marriage, and it was payable in the current coin of the land.[3] Upon her divorce,[4] the wife was entitled to the amount thus secured to her, except in certain cases, hereinafter enumerated.

The amount of the Kethubah above mentioned was the minimum prescribed by law, but it could be indefinitely increased by the husband,[5] and in some instances was increased by law as a punishment for the husband's misconduct.[6] In either case, upon divorcing his wife, the husband was obliged to pay her the full amount, without any diminution, and his entire estate was liable for its payment. There was a case decided by Rabbi Aqiba, where the husband had been ordered to pay the Kethubah to his wife when about to divorce

[1] Sûra 4.
[2] Ibid.
[3] Mishnah Kethuboth xiii, 11; Maimonides' Treatise Ishuth x, 8.
[4] Mishnah Kethuboth vii, 2-5.
[5] Id., v. 1.
[6] Id., v. 7.

her. He had written four hundred zuz in the Kethubah, double the minimum amount provided by law. He objected to paying the full amount of the Kethubah, saying that his father had died leaving an estate of eight hundred zuz to be divided between himself and a brother, and that if he were now obliged to pay to his divorced wife four hundred zuz, the full amount of her Kethubah, it would impoverish him. He offered to pay her two hundred zuz, the minimum provided by law, and to retain the other two hundred zuz which he had inherited. In rendering the decision, Rabbi Aqiba curtly remarked: "You must pay her the whole Kethubah, even if you have to sell the hair off your head."[1]

INCREASE OF THE KETHUBAH.—Under certain circumstances, the Kethubah may be increased by law. If the husband refused his wife her conjugal rights, and at the same time would not divorce her, she was entitled to a divorce; but if she did not choose to demand a divorce, she could remain with him, and he was punished for his default by the addition to her Kethubah of three denarii, or, according to Rabbi Yehudah, three trapiqin, every week.[2]

If the contract or Kethubah contained other stipulations which the husband had undertaken to perform, he was held to a strict and faithful performance of the terms of his obligation. A man having stipulated that he would maintain and sup-

[1] Mishnah Nedarim ix, 5.
[2] Mishnah Kethuboth v, 7.

port the daughter of his wife by a former husband, for a period of five years, divorced his wife before the term had expired; he was, nevertheless, obliged to perform the condition faithfully.[1]

PAYMENT OF THE KETHUBAH.—Where the woman who had not yet attained her majority, had been betrothed and divorced before her marriage had been consummated, the Kethubah was payable to her father, and not to her; but after she had been married, her father lost his authority over her, and upon her divorce the Kethubah was payable to her, and not to him.[2]

Upon payment of the Kethubah, the Get, or Bill of Divorce, was torn crosswise, and the Court wrote on it: "We have torn this Get, not because it is void, but in order that she may not again claim the Kethubah. This woman is permitted to marry again."[3]

As the Kethubah was established for the purpose of protecting the wife against a hasty or ill-advised divorce, all laws concerning it were construed most favorably to her. If she lost the Kethubah and produced the Get, with a statement that the Kethubah had not been paid to her, the court was empowered to award her the minimum dowry prescribed by law, namely, two hundred zuz.

In such cases, as soon as the amount of the Kethubah was paid to her, the Court noted the fact

[1] Mishnah Kethuboth xii, 1.
[2] Id. iv, 2.
[3] Talmud Babli Kethuboth 89 b; Talmud Babli Baba Meçia 18 a.

upon the Get, so that this instrument could not be produced again in support of the woman's claim for the payment of her Kethubah.[1] But in case she had lost the Get, but still had the Kethubah in her possession, and claimed that the amount prescribed therein had not been paid, she could not recover it from her husband. He was simply obliged to set up a plea by way of defence, that he had paid the Kethubah but had lost her receipt for it; in other words, that, as she had lost her Get, he had lost her written acknowledgment of the receipt of the Kethubah, and that, therefore, they were quits. After the Hadrianic revolution under Bar Kokhba, this law was changed. Among the edicts of the Roman authorities intended to suppress the last traces of Jewish national life that remained after the unsuccessful rebellion, was one making it a crime for the Jews to give Bills of Divorce to their wives. This resulted in the practice of destroying the Get immediately after its delivery to the wife, so that its production might not incriminate the parties.[2] Thereupon Rabbi Simon ben Gamaliel decreed that the mere non-production of the Get could not deprive the woman of her right to claim the Kethubah.[3]

In all cases where the husband refused to pay his wife the amount of the Kethubah, she had the right of appeal to the courts, who heard and determined the merits of the case. If the decision was

[1] Mishnah Kethuboth ix, 9.
[2] Infra, page 183.
[3] Mishnah Kethuboth ix, 9.

against the husband and he failed to pay, his lands and goods could be attached and sold by the order of the Court at public sale for the purpose of satisfying her claim. If the estate of the husband was insufficient they proceeded against the estate formerly in his possession, and which was now in the hands of third persons,[1] and until the last Perutah of her dowry was paid, her husband was obliged to support her.[2]

WIFE'S SEPARATE ESTATE.—Upon her divorce the wife was entitled to take possession of the separate estate which she had acquired before or during her marriage. She had the right of disposition, during her marriage, of the separate estate belonging to her before the marriage;[3] but the husband had a usufructuary right in the estate which had come into her possession since her marriage, and she had no power to sell or dispose of it until her marriage was dissolved.[4]

If the husband expended money in improving his wife's separate estate without deriving any benefit or income from it, he was, after he had divorced her, entitled to be repaid the amount thus expended;[5] but if he had derived some income from her estate during their marriage, he lost his right to recover the amount expended by him in improving it, for the law presumed that he took the risk of getting a large or small return for his outlay

[1] Mishnah Gittin v, 2.
[2] Talmud Yerushalmi Baba Meçia sub Mishnah i, 5 (8 a).
[3] Mishnah Kethuboth viii, 1.
[4] Id. viii, 4.
[5] Id. viii, 5.

during their marriage, and nothing if he divorced her.[1] It is very likely that this law also acted as a strong check on the freedom of divorce.

EARNINGS, ETC., OF DIVORCED WIFE.—After the divorce, the separation of the husband and wife was absolute. His power over her and his rights in her estate, her earnings, etc., were at an end, although she still had certain rights against him. Until he had paid her dowry in full she was entitled to be supported by him as though she were still his wife. If she earned or found anything, it belonged to her.[2] It was argued that, inasmuch as she was entitled to retain as her own that which she found and earned, her husband ought to be relieved of the obligation to support her, although he had not yet paid her Kethubah in full; but, said Rabbi Hosh-a'yah (about 220 C. E.), it is to prevent this argument from prevailing that the Mishnah has formally stated the contrary.[3] In fine, she lost none of her rights against him upon being divorced, although he forfeited all and every right that he had against her.

Unless a reconciliation and remarriage took place, her relation to her husband was that of a stranger. If the wife, for three years after her divorce, remained in undisturbed possession of a field belonging to her husband, she could obtain a prescriptive right against him, and the fact that it was his field, and that she had gone into possession

[1] Mishnah Kethuboth viii, 5.
[2] Mishnah Baba Meçia i, 5.
[3] Talmud Yerushalmi Baba Meçia sub Mishnah i, 5 (8 a).

of it during their marriage, made no difference. Her holding over in undisturbed possession after the divorce was like the possession of a stranger, adverse to his claim, and divested him of his title;[1] although, during her marriage, the wife's possession of the husband's property did not affect his title thereto.[2]

Loss of the Kethubah.—The wife's right to claim the amount of her Kethubah depended on her good conduct, and she lost her right in certain cases if she failed in the performance of her duties as a wife. The cases of the adulteress, against whom the law was especially severe,[3] and the woman who had been guilty of antenuptial incontinence,[4] founded on the Biblical laws, were, very probably, the earliest cases in which the woman lost her claim to the Kethubah.

Following these, the Mishnah cites a number of cases in which the woman, by reason of her misconduct, forfeited her right. If she had subjected herself to vows before her marriage, and failed to disclose the fact to her husband, or if she had physical defects which she concealed, she was guilty of fraud, and if her husband divorced her on this account, he was not obliged to pay her the amount of the Kethubah.[5] But it seems that if the physical defects were of such a character that the husband might, by due diligence, have learned

---

[1] Talmud Babli Baba Bathra 47 a.
[2] Talmud Babli Gittin 77 a.
[3] Mishnah Sotah i, 5.
[4] Mishnah Kethuboth i, 2.
[5] Mishnah Qiddushin ii, 5.

of their existence before marrying her, he could not set them up as a pretext for depriving her of the Kethubah;[1] and it was decided that, in any event, the burden of proving that such defects existed before the marriage was upon him.[2]

Generally speaking, the divorced wife lost her Kethubah if she had been guilty of an offense against ethical custom or usage, whether in the breach of some ritualistic prescription or in the violation of some social convention. In either case, however, the offense had to be one involving moral turpitude.

The Mishnah calls these cases breaches of the "Mosaic and Jewish Law," the word Law being used in the sense of usage, custom or mode of living. A distinction is implied in the terms "Mosaic" and "Jewish," the former referring rather to breaches of ritual law, and the latter to offenses against good morals and decency.

Illustrations of breaches of the "Mosaic" law are given in the Mishnah; for instance, if she gave her husband food upon which no tithe had been paid; if she did not set apart the heave offerings; if she broke her vows; or if she submitted to his embraces during the period when she was unclean.

Illustrations of breaches of conventional morality or decency are also there cited, as, for example: If she went abroad bare-headed, with her hair loose; if she sat spinning in the street, or flirted with

[1] Mishnah Kethuboth vii, 8.
[2] Ibid.

strangers; if she cursed her children in her husband's presence (per Abba Saul); or, according to Rabbi Tarphon, if she was noisy, speaking in so loud a tone in her own house that her neighbors could hear her.[1]

The following women also lost their right to the Kethubah on being divorced: The minor who had been given in marriage by her mother or brothers, and who, on attaining her majority, refused to live with her husband; the woman who was related to her husband within the degrees of consanguinity; and the woman who was incapable of bearing children by reason of defects which existed before her marriage, and of which her husband was ignorant.[2]

REFUSAL TO COHABIT WITH HUSBAND.—The woman who denied conjugal rights to her husband was punished by a subtraction of seven denarii a week (or, according to Rabbi Yehudah, seven trapiqin), from her Kethubah, until the entire Kethubah was gone. According to Rabbi Yosé, the deductions were continued until her entire separate estate had been consumed.[3] The Amoraïm decided that the Kethubah could not be diminished until after four weeks' notice had been given to the wife.[4] The court warned her, saying, "Know thou, that even if thy Kethubah amounts to a hundred Mina, thou wilt lose it." Public notice was also given in all synagogues and colleges during this time;

[1] Mishnah Kethuboth vii, 6.
[2] Id. xi, 6.
[3] Id. v, 7.
[4] Talmud Babli Kethuboth 63 b.

after the publication the court again sent her personal notice, warning her that she would lose her Kethubah if she continued to be refractory. If she still persisted, her husband was released from his obligation to support her, and she was given a further period of twelve months to become reconciled to him; and, at the expiration of this period, if the husband divorced her, he was not liable for her Kethubah.[1]

Amemar (flourished 390-420) held that if the wife assigned no reason for her conduct, and acted in a malicious spirit towards her husband, the procedure above mentioned is followed. "But," he said, "if she states that she has an unconquerable aversion to her husband, she is not punished, but may be divorced forthwith, and loses her Kethubah."[2]

The Koran[3] says: "It is not lawful for you to hinder them (women) from marrying others that you may take part of what ye have given them in dowry; unless they have been guilty of manifest crime." It seems that the Mohammedan courts allowed the woman to sue for divorce without forfeiting her dowry. In Babylonia, Jewish women took advantage of the comparative leniency of the Mohammedan law and applied to the Mohammedan courts for divorce from their husbands. It was therefore decreed by Mar Raba, the son of Mar Rab Huna (about 675 C. E.), that women could sue

[1] Talmud Babli Kethuboth 64 a.
[2] Ibid., 63 b. Maimonides' Ishuth xiv, 8.
[3] Koran, Sûra 4.

for divorce without losing their Kethubah, in order to prevent their appeal to the non-Jewish courts for relief.[1] It seems that the leniency of the Mohammedan law was not general; Sale[2] states that the woman suing for divorce usually *lost* her dowry, unless some weighty cause was assigned by her. In Christian countries this decision of Mar Raba was not followed by the Jews, because the Roman law, like the Jewish, deprived the wife of her dowry if she sued for divorce on such ground.[3] Maimonides (1180 C. E.) notes the fact that difference of opinion existed among the Rabbis on this point,[4] and he states[5] the law to be, that the woman suing for divorce on account of an unconquerable aversion to her husband, loses her Kethubah.[6]

DESERTION.—The woman who deserts her husband, by refusing to follow him from one place to another in the same country, or from any country into Palestine, or from any place in Palestine to Jerusalem, loses her right to her Kethubah on being divorced.[7] A woman was not ordinarily obliged to expatriate herself, but was compelled to follow her husband if he removed from one place to another in the same country. Such was the

[1] Opinion of the Gaon Sherira reported in Responsa Gaonim Hemdah Genuzah, Jerusalem 5623. Graetz's "History of the Jews," American Edition, Vol. III, p. 92.
[2] Koran, Preliminary Discourse, Section vi.
[3] Novels of Justinian cxvii, 9.
[4] Maimonides' Treatise Ishuth xiv, 14.
[5] Ibid. xiv, 8.
[6] See also Eben Haëzer lxxvii, 2.
[7] Mishnah Kethuboth xiii, 10–11.

position of the land of Palestine (commonly called the Holy Land) and the City of Jerusalem (commonly called the Holy City) in the mind and affections of the ancient Hebrews, that a removal from any country into Palestine, or from any city in Palestine or elsewhere to Jerusalem, was not deemed an expatriation, but rather a return home. The wife was not obliged to leave Jerusalem or Palestine under any penalty, but was deprived of her right to her Kethubah if she refused to remove thither with her husband.[1]

THE CUSTODY AND MAINTENANCE OF THE CHILDREN OF THE DIVORCED WOMAN.—When Hagar was sent away out of the house of Abraham, her son Ishmael was sent with her,[2] not because she was entitled to have him, but because he was offensive to Sarah, who feared that he might be allowed to share in the inheritance with her son Isaac.[3] Had Abraham chosen to keep his son while sending away the mother, he would have exercised an undoubted right; for, under the constitution of the patriarchal household, children were the legal property of the father, and the mother had no right whatever to their custody.

But the same influences that modified the legal status of the wife and entitled her to demand and receive a divorce from her husband, affected her rights with respect to her children, and in Talmudic times she seems to have had stronger rights than

[1] Talmud Babli Kethuboth 110 b; and see supra, p. 73.
[2] Genesis xxi, 14.
[3] Id. 10.

her husband to their custody. The first regulations concerning the custody of the children of the divorced woman appear to have been made during the early Mishnic period, and relate exclusively to the charge and care of sucklings.

The question became the subject of dispute between the Schools of Hillel and Shammai. The School of Shammai, who were the rigorists, declared that when the wife had made a vow to abstain from giving suck to her child, her vow was binding on her and she could not be compelled to nurse the child. The School of Hillel were of the opinion that her vow was null and void, and that her maternal duty was paramount,[1] but that if she had been divorced she could not be compelled to nurse the child.[2] After the mother had been divorced, and was willing, as was most natural, to suckle her child, she was entitled to be paid for her services,[3] and her former husband was obliged to give her especial care and attention and such extra food as her condition required;[4] but if she was unwilling to nurse it, she could not be compelled to do so.[5] If, however, the child recognizing its mother, was unwilling to take nourishment from any other woman, she was compelled to nurse it,[6] and her former husband was obliged to maintain her until the child was weaned, *i. e.*, for a period of at least two

[1] Talmud Babli Kethuboth 59 b.
[2] Ibid.
[3] Ibid.
[4] Talmud Babli Kethuboth 65 b.
[5] Ibid. 59 b.
[6] Ibid.

years.¹ A case of this kind came before Mar Samuel bar Abba (160-257 C. E.) known in the Talmud as Samuel of Nahardea, in Babylonia. His decision was reached in characteristic Oriental style. The mother having been divorced, had vowed not to nurse her child. He ordered her to take her place in a row of women and the child was borne into the room. The child regarded its mother longer than any of the other women, and she being overcome with confusion dropped her eyes. "Raise your eyes," sententiously said the Rabbi, "and take your child."²

The earliest Rabbinical regulations on record regarding the custody of children who were no longer nurslings are the decisions of Rabbis Assi, of Palestine, and Ulla and Ḥasda, of Babylonia. Their decisions were rendered contemporaneously with the publication of a Constitution of the Emperors Diocletian and Maximian (end of third century C. E.), which provided that, after the divorce of the parents, the judge could award the custody of the children according to his discretion, and was not compelled to give the males to the father and the females to the mother.³

Rabbi Assi decided that after the period of nursing had elapsed, if the divorced woman desired to keep her son, she was entitled to his custody until his sixth year.⁴ Rabbi Ulla decided

¹ Talmud Babli Kethuboth 60 a. This opinion was adopted by Mohammed. Koran, Sûras 2 and 65.
² Talmud Babli Kethuboth 60 a.
³ Code of Justinian, Book v, Title xxiv, Const. i.
⁴ Talmud Babli Kethuboth 65 b.

that, in the meantime, the husband was liable for his maintenance and support,[1] and Rabbi Hasda decided that the mother was entitled to the custody of her daughter without regard to her age.[2]

The result of these decisions was that both the female and the male children were given to the mother, but the custody of the boys could be claimed by the father after their sixth year. It was optional with the divorced mother to retain the custody of her children after they were weaned. If she could not or would not keep them, the husband was obliged to receive them, and if he had died in the meantime, they became wards of the congregation.[3] The later law seems to have gone back to the old rule of the Roman law, giving the Court the power in the first instance to award the custody of the children of the divorced couple according to its discretion.[4]

The duty of the father to support his children who are in the custody of his divorced wife is established at Roman law by a novel of Justinian (about 550 C. E.), which provided that the legal rights of the children and their rights to alimentation by the father, should in no way be impaired by a divorce; that if the divorce was given by the wife to her husband because of his fault, she could retain the custody of the children who were to be maintained at the expense of the father, but if the

[1] Talmud Babli Kethuboth 65 b.
[2] Talmud Babli Kethuboth 102 b.
[3] Maimonides' Ishuth xxi, 18.
[4] Rabbi Isserles to Eben Haëzer lxxxii, 7.

mother was the guilty one, the father had the right of custody; and if he was poor and the mother rich, the burden of maintaining the children should fall on her.[1]

At Jewish law, under the decision of Rabbi Ulla,[2] the father was obliged to maintain his son while in the custody of the divorced wife until he reached the age of six years. Thereafter, if the mother refused to give the child up to the father, the latter was no longer liable for his support;[3] but the daughter must always be supported by her father.[4] If, however, the father was dead and the mother was unwilling or unable to support the children, they became wards of the congregation, and were supported out of the public fund.[5]

[1] Novels of Justinian, cxvii, 7.
[2] Supra, p. 129.
[3] Maimonides' Ishuth xxi, 17.
[4] Ibid.
[5] Maimonides' Ishuth xxi, 18, et supra, p. 130.

CHAPTER XI.

THE BILL OF DIVORCE (GET).

Antiquity of the Bill of Divorce—Supposed by Rabbinical Writers to have been known to Abraham—Peculiar to the Jews—Arabian Form of Divorce.—Form of Divorce among Greeks and Romans—Bills of Divorce prepared in the non-Jewish Courts.

ANTIQUITY OF THE BILL OF DIVORCE.—The form of the bill of divorce mentioned in Deuteronomy, and the formalities attending its delivery are unknown. By analogy to known forms of legal procedure of very ancient times, it has been supposed that the giving of the bill of divorce was a formal act, done in the presence of the Elders at the "gate" of the City.[1] This, however, is mere conjecture; and there is reason to believe that the reverse is true. For this giving of the bill of divorce was simply the exercise by the husband of his right to send away his wife "if she find no favor in his eyes;" and it is not to be supposed that the procedure in such cases was assimilated to the formal transactions between strangers or between members of different families. The oldest form of divorce was probably the simplest, and the complex formalities attending the prepa-

[1] Deuteronomy xxii, 15.

(132)

ration and delivery of the Bill of Divorce are of comparatively late origin.

The form of divorce used by Abraham seems to have been simple enough. "And Abraham arose in the morning, and he took bread, and a bottle of water, and he gave it unto Hagar, putting it on her shoulder, and the child, and sent her away."[1]

A late rabbinical tradition[2] tells that Sarah requested Abraham to send Hagar away by writing a Bill of Divorce for her, and that Abraham arose in the morning and sent her away with a Bill of Divorce in her hand.[3]

But it may be assumed, despite this tradition, that as long as the patriarchal family was nomadic and never in permanent contact with other families, the simple "sending away" was sufficient as an act of divorce. When the herdsmen became agriculturists, with fixed habitations, new conditions arose which gradually changed the ancient forms of legal procedure.

With the general introduction of the art of writing, in all probability came the Bill of Divorce as the best means of proving the legal act, and as evidence of the right of the wife to contract a second marriage.[4]

The Bill of Divorce had been in use for so long a time in Israel that the memory of man did not run to the contrary, and the people could conceive

---

[1] Genesis xxi, 14.
[2] Pirqé di Rabbi Eliezer, Cap. 30.
[3] Yalkut Shimeoni Genesis, Sec. 95.
[4] Talmud Yerushalmi Qiddushin sub Mishnah i, 5 (60 c).

of no period when it had not been in use; hence they believed that even Abraham was already entirely familiar with the complicated divorce procedure of the later times. The patriarch Abraham fills so large a space in the background of Jewish history, that the people readily ascribed to him supernatural wisdom and all-embracing knowledge, even supposing him to have performed all the commandments of the Torah, although the Torah had not yet been revealed in his day.[1]

Rabbinical literature contains other traditions assigning a very great age to the introduction of the Bill of Divorce.

The Zohar records a tradition that it was a custom in Israel for the soldiers of King David going to war to give Bills of Divorce to their wives, in order to free them from the Levirate marriage in case their husbands died in battle.[2]

The Mekhilta states that the bondwoman who had been elevated to be a lawful wife[3] could not be sent away without a Bill of Divorce.[4]

It is undoubtedly true that the Bill of Divorce is of very great antiquity among the Jews. The great unknown prophet of the captivity (about 550 B. C. E.), whose writings are attached to the Book of Isaiah, forming chapters forty to sixty-six, incidentally mentions the Bill of Divorce as something

[1] Talmud Yerushalmi Qiddushin sub Mishnah iv, 12 (66 d).
[2] Zohar, Exodus 107 a. See also Talmud Babli Kethuboth 9 b.
[3] Exodus xxi, 7-11.
[4] Mekhilta Mishpatim, Sec. 3. See also Talmud Babli Sanhedrin 22 a.

well known. "Where is the Bill of Divorce of your mother," he says, "wherewith I have sent her away?"[1] In the Book of Deuteronomy[2] the Bill of Divorce is also mentioned incidentally as an established institution well known among the people.

THE BILL OF DIVORCE PECULIARLY A JEWISH FORM OF SEPARATION.—The giving of a Bill of Divorce to the wife was a custom peculiar to the Hebrews, and the heathen nations round about the Jews did not give Bills of Divorce to their wives when they sent them away.[3]

Rabbi Yoḥanan (199-279 C. E.) states that the heathen gave no Bill of Divorce when they sent away their wives; they simply divorced each other by separating without formality.[4]

The Jewish woman who was divorced was not recognized as such by any change in her appearance, but established the fact by the production of her Get (Bill of Divorce); the heathen woman, however, was, according to Rabbi Huna, recognized as divorced when she appeared on the street with her head uncovered;[5] for the married heathen woman never appeared uncovered except when she left the *manus* of her husband.[6]

Rabbi Aḥa[7] calls attention to the fact that in

[1] Isaiah l, 1.
[2] Deuteronomy xxiv, 1-4.
[3] Talmud Yerushalmi Qiddushin sub Mishnah i, 1 (58 c); Yalkut Shimeoni Malachi, Sec. 589.
[4] Talmud Yerushalmi, Ibid.
[5] Talmud Babli Sanhedrin 58 b.
[6] Maimonides' Treatise Melakhim ix, 8.
[7] Talmud Yerushalmi Qiddushin sub Mishnah 1, 1 (58 c).

the Book of the Prophecy of Malachi the Deity is always spoken of as *Yahveh* and *Yahveh Çebhaoth* (Lord of Hosts) except in one passage,[1] where his name is mentioned in connection with divorce; there he is called *Yahveh Elohê Yisrael* (the Lord God of Israel); and the Rabbi concludes that this is because the heathen nations do not have the formality of the Bill of Divorce, which is a peculiar custom of the Hebrews.[2]

I have not been able to ascertain whether the ancient Babylonians and Persians, among whom the Jews dwelt, made use of a written Bill of Divorce; the ancient Arabians, as well as the Greeks and Romans, with all of whom the Jews had close relations, had no Bill of Divorce.

ARABIAN FORM OF DIVORCE.—Among those ancient Arabian tribes that lived under a system in which kinship was traced through the females, the husband did not bring his wife to live with him, but went to live with her and her kin. In divorcing her, he did not send her away, for she was at home and he was the stranger. He used a formula which indicated that he left her and went back to his own folk, saying: "Begone! I will no longer drive thy flocks to the pasture."[3]

This form of divorce was unlawful among the Hebrews. The Rabbis declared it void, and pointed out the essential difference between the principles of the Hebrew and the heathen marriage and divorce.

[1] Malachi ii, 16.
[2] Midrash Rabba Bereshith, Cap. xviii.
[3] W. Robertson Smith, "Kinship and Marriage in Early Arabia," p. 94.

Mar Samuel expresses it as follows: "When an Israelite marries, he gives his bride a piece of silver or some other object, and uses some such formula as, 'thou art sanctified unto me,' 'thou art betrothed unto me,' or 'thou art a wife unto me;' and if he says, 'I am thy husband,' or 'I am thy betrothed,' she is not then betrothed to him.

"Likewise, in divorcing his wife, he gives her the Get (Bill of Divorce), saying, 'Thou art sent away,' 'thou art divorced,' or 'thou art allowed to any man.' If, however, he says, 'I am not thy husband,' or 'I am not thy betrothed,' this is no valid divorce, because at Jewish law the husband *takes* a wife and does not *give himself* to her; he *sends* her away, but does not *withdraw himself* from her."[1]

Among the Bedouins the common formula of divorce was: "She was my slipper and I cast her off."[2] Another form of divorce among the early Arabs was the formula: "Thou art to me as the back of my mother."[3] This was the most solemn form known to them. In the eye of the law, the wife who was thus divorced became the mother of her former husband, and, like his own mother, was forever thereafter prohibited from remarrying him or any of his kinsmen who were within the degrees of consanguinity or affinity which would have prevented them from marrying his true mother.

Mohammed put an end to the fictitious relation-

[1] Talmud Babli Qiddushin 5 b.
[2] Burckhart, "Bedouins," i, 113.
[3] W. Robertson Smith, "Kinship and Marriage in Early Arabia," p. 164.

ship thus created. "God hath not . . . made your wives (some of whom ye divorce, regarding them thereafter as your mothers) your true mothers" . . . . "this is your saying in your mouths; but God speaketh the truth, and he directeth the right way."[1] But Mohammed expressly declared his own wives to be inviolate, saying: "The prophet is nigher unto the true believers than their own souls; and *his wives are their mothers.*" . . . "It is not fit for you to give any uneasiness to the prophet of God, or to marry his wives after him forever."[2] It likewise appears that the divorced wife of a Jewish king was not allowed to remarry.[3]

FORM OF DIVORCE AMONG THE GREEKS AND ROMANS.—Among the Greeks as well as the Romans either the husband or the wife could divorce the other. Technically the divorce of the wife by her husband was "ἀποπομπή" (sending away) and the divorce of the husband by the wife "ἀπόλειψις" (leaving). The woman could not *send away* her husband because she had been brought into his house from which she could not, of course, eject him, but she could *leave* his house and go back to her own kin.[4] The free marriage could be easily dissolved by either party. "Farewell," says Alcmene to Jupiter, whom she supposes to be her husband Amphitryon, "take your property, return

[1] Koran (Sale's translation), Sûra 33.
[2] Koran, Ibid.
[3] Talmud Yerushalmi Sanhedrin sub Mishnah ii, 3 (20 a).
[4] Selden, "De jure Naturali et Gentium juxta disciplinam Ebræorum," Book v, Chap. 7.

mine to me."[1] This was the customary formula, "tuas res tibi habeto,"[2] "τὰ σεαυτῆς πράττε[3] and was very like the old formula in use among the Hebrews. "T'le Khethubekh uçeï"[4] "Take thy dowry and go." The divorce was usually accompanied by some act indicative of the separation, such as giving back the dowry, taking away the keys from the wife and the like.

The religious marriage by *confarreatio* was not so easily dissolved, and could only be destroyed by a *contrarius actus*, namely *diffarcatio*. "The husband and wife who wished to separate appeared for the last time before the common hearth; a priest and witnesses were present. As on the day of marriage, a cake of wheaten flour was presented to the husband and wife. But instead of sharing it between them they rejected it. Then instead of prayers, they pronounced formulas of a strange, severe, spiteful, frightful character, a sort of malediction by which the wife renounced the worship and gods of her husband. From that moment the religious bond was broken. The community of worship having ceased, every other common interest ceased to exist and the marriage was dissolved."[5] The Bill of Divorce was not introduced at Rome until the reign of Augustus (27 B.C.E. to 14 C.E.),[6] or, according to another authority, until the reign of

[1] Plautus, "Amphitryon," Act iii, Sc. ii.
[2] Digest, Book xxiv, Title ii, Fragment ii, Sec. i.
[3] Selden, "Uxor Ebraica," iii, 27.
[4] Talmud Babli Kethuboth 82 b.
[5] De Coulanges, "The Ancient City," p. 60.
[6] Hunter, "Roman Law," Ed. 1876, p. 510.

Diocletian (284-305 C.E.)[1] The latter seems to be the better opinion, and corresponds with an interesting fact derived from Jewish sources. Among the edicts of the Emperor Hadrian was one forbidding the granting of Bills of Divorce by Jewish men to their wives. This was one of the measures used to utterly destroy the last remnants of Jewish life and manners, after the rebellion under Bar Kokhba.[2] It is unlikely that the Roman authorities would have considered the Bill of Divorce a Jewish institution like the Sabbath and Circumcision, if it had been in use also among the Romans. It is probable therefore that is was not introduced at Rome until the reign of Diocletian,[3] about 150 years after Hadrian.

This recognition of the Bill of Divorce as an institution peculiar to the Hebrews is furthermore emphasized by the decision of the Rabbis that a Bill of Divorce granted to the wife upon her appeal to a non-Jewish court was invalid.[4]

The principle governing the legal relations of Jews and non-Jews is summed up in the dictum of Mar Samuel: *"Dina d'malkhuthe dina"* (the law of the kingdom is the law).[5] In matters affecting their intercourse with the non-Jewish people among whom they lived, the Jews gladly submitted

[1] Mackeldey " Roman Law," (Dropsie's Edition), Sec. 577, note 7.
[2] Graetz's " History of the Jews," Vol. II, p. 422.
[3] See also Rabbinowicz, " Legislation Civile du Thalmud," Vol. I, Introduction, p. 33, etc.
[4] Mishnah Gittin, i, 5.
[5] Talmud Babli Baba Qama 113 a.

THE BILL OF DIVORCE. 141

to the lawfully constituted authorities, obeying the law of the land and demanding its protection. But religious or quasi-religious matters were determinable only by their own Jewish tribunals, who were learned in the Jewish law. All contracts, or instruments affecting legal rights which were common to Jews and non-Jews and were prepared in the non-Jewish courts, as well as all decrees made by their authority, were accepted as binding by all Jewish tribunals, and the Jewish law gave them full faith and credit and acknowledged their obligation. But Bills of Divorce, being peculiar to the Jews, were governed only by Jewish law, and the Rabbis maintained their independence in such matters by declaring the Bill of Divorce issuing out of the Court of the Gentiles to be void.[1]

In the seventh century C.E., when Jewish women sought to obtain Bills of Divorce from their husbands in the Mohammedan courts, the Rabbis declared them null and void, and for the purpose of putting an end to this practice without coming into conflict with the secular authorities, they gave certain new rights and privileges to the Jewish women who appeared as plaintiffs, thereby making the appeals to the Mohammedan courts unnecessary.

[1] Talmud Babli Gittin 10 b.
[2] Graetz's "History of the Jews," American Edition, Vol. III, p. 92, supra p. 59.

CHAPTER XII.

PREPARING THE BILL OF DIVORCE (GET).

Divorce Procedure, at first Simple, Became Complex—Husband Must Give the Order to Prepare the Get with the Intention of Divorcing His Wife—What is Deemed a Sufficient Order to the Scribe and Witnesses—Exceptions in Favor of Persons in Situation of Danger, etc.—Uses of the Bill of Divorce—Divorce by a Mute Husband—Writing the Get—The Scribe—Fees of the Scribe—The Writing Materials.

IT has been suggested, in another place, that the complicated system of procedure among the Jews acted as a check on the theoretically unrestricted right of the husband to divorce his wife at his pleasure. Divorce procedure, at first simple and finally complex, has followed the natural and common course of all systems of law and legal practice. The refinements of Pleading at Common Law, the involved phraseology and technical prolixity of a deed of conveyance are instances in point. Cautious lawyers noted the ambiguities and resultant disputes due to loosely drawn instruments and to insure against these, gradually evolved complex technical forms. By following these forms exactness of meaning, as established by the legal use of terms, is secured, and a large amount of error and dispute is eliminated from the transactions. It is true that lawyers are required to perform the service of preparing the proper papers, and the layman who attempts to do so for himself, is apt to fall into a sea of trouble. It was not the purpose of the lawyers and judges, in gradually arriving at the modern forms, to make business for the profession and to throw legal matters in the hands of a class of specially trained men, although that was undoubtedly one of the results of their work. By their technicalities they sought exactness and the avoidance of dispute and litigation.

The rules of Divorce Procedure at Jewish law promoted exactness, minimized mistake and misunderstanding, and settled with reasonable certainty the legal status and the mutual obligations and rights of the parties. The result of this system was to make the granting of a Bill of Divorce too difficult for any layman to undertake, and the matter being thrown into the hands of the Judge or Rabbi, the difficulty of divorce was enhanced, because the weight of Rabbinical persuasive power was thrown against it. Men were cautioned to beware of attempting to give Bills of Divorce unless they were well versed in the law, lest they cause trouble and disgrace[1] and some Rabbis were of the opinion that all Bills of Divorce prepared by laymen ought to be declared null and void.

ORDERING THE PREPARATION AND DELIVERY OF THE GET.—The first step in the Procedure was the order given by the husband to the proper persons to write and deliver the Get (Bill of

[1] Talmud Babli Qiddushin 6 a.

Divorce). They thereby became his agents, and according to the common principle of law they could not, by their acts, exceed the power granted them. If they were told to write the Get they could do this and nothing more; if they were told to write and deliver it, they might act accordingly. In a case where a man had given the order, "write a Get for my wife," it was held that a delivery to her of the instrument was unauthorized and void; but that if from subsequent events it appeared that it was truly the husband's intention to divorce her, his intention could be carried out despite this technical irregularity.[1] The husband having given the order to write the Get, went up to the roof of his house for the purpose of attending to some matter there, and falling over the edge, was killed. The Get having been written and *delivered* to the wife, the question arose whether the delivery was lawful and the woman divorced from him, or whether, the delivery of the Get being unauthorized, she was his widow. The determination of this question affected the property rights of the woman in her husband's estate; it also settled the question of the Levirate marriage, for under the Biblical law[2] the widow having no children was obliged to marry her deceased husband's brother, and could only be released from this obligation by the performance of the ceremony of Haliça.[3] This case having

[1] Mishnah Gittin vi, 6.
[2] Deuteronomy xxv, 5–10.
[3] So called from the ceremony of drawing off the shoe. See Deuteronomy xxv, 9.

been brought before Rabbi Simon ben Gamaliel (died about 169 C. E.), he decided that the question of the husband's intention not being determined by his order, was to be determined by the manner in which the accident occurred. If he fell off the roof accidentally, as for instance, if a gust of wind blew him over, it could not be presumed that he had intended to divorce her when he said "write a Get," and she will be deemed his widow; but if he threw himself off the roof with suicidal intent, it must be presumed that he had ordered the Get for his wife in contemplation of his death, and that the words used by him in giving the order must be liberally construed, because in his agitation he may have forgotten to fully express his purpose in proper words.[1]

If the husband in the above case, instead of merely saying, "write a Get for my wife," had said "write a Get and give it to my wife," or "write a letter of divorce and give it to her," or "divorce her," or had made use of some such expression to indicate that it was his desire that the Get should not merely be written, but should also be delivered, there would have been no doubt as to the decision that she was divorced.[2] If he had merely used such expressions as "release her," provide for her," "do unto her as is customary," or "do unto her as is proper," it appears that, under the construction given by the Rabbis to these terms, they would constitute no lawful warrant for a scribe and the

[1] Mishnah Gittin vi, 6.
[2] Mishnah Gittin vi, 5.

witnesses to attend to the writing and delivery of the Get.[1]

To this rule there were several exceptions made in favor of persons who, while in situations of great danger, did not express their intention with technical exactness. In addition to the case above mentioned, the Mishnah cites the case of one who, being led to execution, ordered a Get to be written, without adding that it should be delivered to his wife. It was, nevertheless, held to be valid, upon the presumption that his agitation, in face of death, caused him to forget to add the words.[2] This principle, that the strict law will be relaxed in favor of one who makes a statement, or performs an act, in contemplation of death, was a very ancient one, and in the report of the above case, the Mishnah indicates its antiquity by stating that it was the rule "in the beginning." Later on, the principle was extended to cover the case of one who was about to go on a voyage beyond the sea, or on a journey in a caravan through the desert. The reason for the rule in these cases differed, however, from that of the case of the man led to execution. At Jewish law, absence gave no warrant for presumption of death; if, perchance, the husband, having gone abroad, should die, and no direct evidence of his death be obtainable, his wife could never remarry, and would be placed in the anomalous position of being a wife and a widow at the same time. She was known as Eguna, or "the

[1] Mishnah Gittin vi, 5.
[2] Ibid.

chained one," and the law was mercifully relaxed in order to prevent so unfortunate a condition of the wife.

Still later, the principle was extended to include the case of one who is dangerously ill; the reason in this case being similar to that assigned in the case of the man who is being led to execution.[1]

If one, who had fallen into a pit, cried out, calling upon any one within sound of his voice to write a Get for his wife, but not adding that it should also be delivered to her, it would, nevertheless, upon the principle above cited, be valid if written and delivered.[2]

From the citation of these cases, it will be seen that the Bill of Divorce could be used, and very probably was often used, for the purpose of saving the wife from being an Eguna, or for the purpose of saving her from the Levirate marriage, whereby she would have been compelled, if childless, to marry her husband's brother, if he, the brother, so desired. The husband *in conspectu mortis* delivered or ordered the delivery of the Get to his wife, whereby she became a free woman and was not amenable to the law of the Yebama.[3]

It was essential that the husband himself should order the Get to be written and delivered to the wife.[4] In the case of a man who had been stricken

[1] Mishnah Gittin vi, 5; Mishnah Tebul Yom iv, 5.
[2] Mishnah Gittin vi, 6.
[3] Yebama was the technical name of the widow who was bound by the law (Deuteronomy xxv., 5-10) to marry her deceased husband's brother; the brother was known as the Yabam.
[4] Mishnah Gittin vii, 2.

dumb, and who, therefore, could not order the document to be prepared, it was permissible to write a Get and deliver it upon his order, given by signs or gestures. The deaf-mute could not divorce at all.[1]

For the purpose of arriving at the intention of the mute, he was asked whether he desired the Get to be prepared; he assented by nodding his head. Thereupon he was tested by a series of questions, three times repeated, for the purpose of determining whether he fully understood what was to be done.[2]

An ancient formula for thus determining the mental soundness of the mute is given in the Talmud. The witnesses asked him, "Shall we write a Get for your wife?" He nods affirmatively. "Shall we direct it to your mother?" He nods his head negatively. "Shall we direct it to your wife?" He nods his head affirmatively. "Shall we direct it to your sister?" He nods his head negatively, etc.[3]

WRITING THE GET.—THE SCRIBE.—All persons were qualified to act as scribes in the preparation of the Get, even those who were otherwise legally disqualified, such as a deaf-mute, an idiot or an infant. These, however, could perform the duty of scribes only under the supervision of a competent person.[4] The act of writing was merely a ministe-

---

[1] Supra, page 51.
[2] Mishnah Gittin vii, 1.
[3] Talmud Yerushalmi sub Mishnah Gittin vii, 1 (48 c. d.).
[4] Talmud Babli Gittin 23 a.

rial duty, and, therefore, could be performed by any one, under the direction of those, whose duty it was to take care that the Get be written in proper form according to law.[1] The woman who was about to be divorced could write her own Get, and after giving it to her husband and having it redelivered to her by him, she was divorced. The mere writing of the Get was a matter of minor importance, the validity of the Get being established by the subscribing witnesses.[2]

Bills of Divorce which were prepared in the courts of the heathen were invalid, for reasons above given.[3] This discrimination against non-Jewish courts extended only to the cases of Bills of Divorce and Bills of Manumission of slaves. All other documents prepared in the courts of the Gentiles were received at Jewish law as though they had been prepared in a Jewish court. The rules of law applicable to Bills of Manumission are similar to those applicable to Bills of Divorce in three classes of cases—when the documents were prepared in a non-Jewish court, when they were witnessed by a Samaritan (Kuthi), and when they were delivered.[4]

If it be borne in mind that originally both the slave and the wife were members of the husband's *familia*, and equally subject to the *patria potestas*, the reason for the close analogy in procedure be-

[1] Mishnah Gittin ii, 5; Mishnah Eduyoth ii, 3.
[2] Ibid.
[3] Supra, page 59.
[4] Talmud Babli Gittin 9 a.

tween the two cases will become apparent. The master, by manumitting his slave or divorcing his wife, rendered them equally *sui juris*, and thereby forever removed them from under his power and control. Thus the original similarity in the status of the slave and the wife left its impress on the law centuries thereafter, and we have in the case above cited an instance where they are classed together for apparently no other reason than this ancient similarity. The courts of the heathen could not grant a bill of divorce, because this was a quasi-religious institution, and one, therefore, over which a non-Jewish court could exercise no jurisdiction. This reason cannot be assigned for the law that a non-Jewish court could not prepare a valid bill of manumission of a slave, more especially since all the Rabbis agreed that in all other cases the documents prepared by the non-Jewish courts were absolutely valid and binding, although they were written and attested by non-Jews.[1] We are, therefore, forced to the conclusion that the ancient similarity in the status of wife and slave was the reason for the later analogy between the Bill of Divorce and the Bill of Manumission.

There was at least one doctor of high authority, Rabbi Simon ben Yohai, who was of the opinion that even bills of divorce and of manumission prepared in the courts of the heathen are valid, and that their validity could only be brought into

[1] Mishnah Gittin i, 4.

question if the person preparing them was an ἰδιώτης.[1]

It was essential that the scribe should receive the order directly from the husband. In a case where the husband was asked, "Shall we write a Get to your wife?" and assented, and thereupon the person who had received the order from him instructed third persons to write and witness the Get, it was declared to be void, and although this Get was given to the husband by the scribe, and he himself delivered it to his wife, it was, nevertheless, invalid, because it was a rule of law that the husband himself must give the order to the scribe to write it and to the witnesses to attest.[2] The person whom the husband constituted his agent could not delegate his power to another; but Rabbi Ḥanina, of the town of Ono, declared that if the husband gave his directions to three men to give the Get to his wife, they could order another to write it; because, being three, they were looked upon as a Beth Din,[3] or court, and as such had the authority to appoint a scribe to prepare documents to which they afterwards gave validity.[4]

Although this decision was given upon the

[1] Mishnah Gittin i, 5. The Mishnah uses the term "Hediot," a layman. Rabbinowicz ("Leg. Civ. du Thalmud," Vol. I, p. 333) takes it to mean an illiterate person.

[2] Mishnah Gittin vii, 1.

[3] A court of law for the trial of civil suits consisted of three members, one chosen by the plaintiff, one by the defendant, and the third by these two (Mishnah Sanhedrin iii, 1), practically a court of arbitration.

[4] Mishnah Gittin vi, 7.

authority of so distinguished a doctor as Rabbi Aqiba,[1] it did not become law. Against it the Mishnah cites the opinion of Rabbi Yosé, who said with much emphasis: "We have received a tradition that even if a man directs the great Sanhedrin at Jerusalem (the highest tribunal of the Jewish state) to give a Get to his wife, they cannot delegate the office of preparing the Get to another; and if it be," adds Rabbi Yosé, in rather a peppery manner, "that the Sanhedrin do not know how to write it (if they are not skilled scribes), let them learn, and then write and deliver the Get accordingly."[2]

As stated above, the scribe had to be specially requested, or ordered by the husband, to write the Get, and if some one other than the husband gave the order, it was null and void.

If the husband instructed more than one to prepare the Get, all of those asked had to unite, and

[1] The Mishnah at this place states that Rabbi Ḥanina brought this law from prison. Rashi in his Commentary states that Rabbi Aqiba is the authority for it, he having given it to Rabbi Ḥanina during his incarceration. Aqiba had taken a prominent part in the last heroic attempt made by the Jews, during the reign of the Emperor Hadrian, to throw off the Roman yoke (about 135 C. E.), and after the defeat of the Jewish arms, Aqiba and many others of the most distinguished leaders were imprisoned and executed (Graetz's "History of the Jews," Vol. II, p. 428). While he was in prison, many of his disciples, in disguise and in danger of their lives, visited him for the purpose of consulting his opinion on questions of law (Talmud Yerushalmi Yebamoth sub Mishnah xii, 5 (12 d).

[2] Mishnah Gittin vi, 7.

PREPARING THE BILL OF DIVORCE. 153

a mere majority did not suffice. If, for instance, a man said to ten people, "Write a Get and give it to my wife," one of them wrote it and two signed as attesting witnesses, in the presence of all of them; but if the husband specifically ordered all of them to write it, they were all obliged to sign the document as attesting witnesses. Hence in the case where all were requested to sign and one died before signing, the Get was declared void.[1]

FEES OF THE SCRIBE.—It was the rule of the Mishnah that the husband pay the fee of the scribe for preparing the Bill of Divorce.[2] The theory being, that the divorce was an act done to the advantage of the husband and at his special request. On the same principle, the borrower paid the scribe's fee for the preparation of the document, showing his indebtedness; so also, the tenant paid the fee for preparing the lease, and the purchaser for preparing a deed of sale.

In each of the above cases, the party to whose advantage the transaction was presumed to be made, was charged with the payment of the scribe's fee. But in the course of the development of the law in Babylonia, the theory in this particular instance underwent a complete change. It was then decided[3] that the fees of the scribe were to be paid by the wife.

This was a Rabbinical innovation for the purpose of preventing the husband from setting up the

[1] Mishnah Gittin vi, 7.
[2] Mishnah Baba Bathra x, 3.
[3] Talmud Babli Baba Bathra 168 a.

question of expense as an excuse for the non-delivery of the Get. Presumably, this innovation was first introduced in cases where the husband was about to desert his wife, and where it was, no doubt, to her advantage that the divorce should be granted. Later on the distinction between the respective positions of the parties was lost and it was made a rule that the wife should pay the fees of the scribe in all cases.[1]

THE WRITING MATERIALS.—Much space is devoted in the Talmud to discussions about the proper materials to be used in the preparation of a Get; some of them occasioned by questions of practical importance which were brought before the Rabbis for decision, and others merely the result of their love of theoretical speculation. The sum and substance of all these discussions is summarized in one sentence of the Mishnah. The Get may be written on any material whatever and with any substance which leaves a permanent mark.[2]

Rabbi Yosé, the Galilean, was of the opinion that a Get could not be written on anything animate or edible.[3] This rather remarkable dictum was the result of a curious discussion upon the validity of a Get written on the horn of a cow. The question of the validity of the Get written on the hand of a slave also arose.[4] Rabbi Yehudah ben Bathyra, of Babylonia, was of the opinion that

[1] Maimonides' Treatise Gerushin ii, 4.
[2] Mishnah Gittin ii, 3.
[3] Ibid.
[4] The reader will be reminded of Mr. Meeson's Will, in Mr. Rider Haggard's novel of that title.

a Get could not be written on papyrus which had been previously used and the writing on which had been erased (palimpsest), nor on unfinished vellum, because in such cases forgery would be easy. But the general opinion was that it made no difference on what material the Get was written, provided that it was properly written and delivered to the wife in the presence of witnesses.[1]

The Get could not be written on anything attached to the soil, unless the article had been previously severed from the ground, for the reason that it would be necessary, after the Get had been written, to cut it off from the ground, before delivering it to the wife, and this would be in defiance of the law that nothing must be done to the document between the writing and delivery.[2]

[1] Mishnah Gittin ii, 4.
[2] Ibid.

CHAPTER XIII.

THE FORM OF THE BILL OF DIVORCE (GET) AND THE GET "ON CONDITION."

Maimonides' Form—Blank Forms—The Folded Get—The Essentials of a Get—Date—*Dies juridici*—Names—Words of Separation—Clauses in Restraint of Marriage—The Get " On Condition "—Origin of the Right of the Husband to Annex Conditions to his Bill of Divorce—Wife Could Accept or Reject—Condition Must be Strictly Complied With—On Condition of the Husband's Death—On Condition of his Failure to Return.

FROM the scattered references in the Mishnah it is possible to re-construct, with fair accuracy, the ancient form of the Get, although it cannot be determined when this particular form came into use. The original form of the Get was very probably much more simple than the one in use at the end of the period of the Mishnah, and the later and more complicated form was gradually evolved under the decision of the judges in particular cases, to meet the new requirements of the law. Maimonides[1] gives the following form, which in his day (at the end of the twelfth century of the present era) was already known as a very ancient form. It corresponds very largely to the hypothetical form which might be reconstructed from the fragmen-

[1] Treatise Gerushin iv, 12.

FORM OF BILL OF DIVORCE. 157

tary references of the Mishnah; with some slight changes it has been in uninterrupted use for about two thousand years, being used to this very day.[1] "On the........day of the week and........day of the month of........in the year....... since the creation of the world[2] (or of the era of the Seleucidæ),[3] the era according to which we are accustomed to reckon in this place, to wit, the town of........[4] do I........the son of........[5] of the town of........[6] (and by whatever other name or surname I[7] or my father may be known, and my town and his town)[8] thus determine, being of sound mind[9] and under no constraint;[10] and I do release and send away and put aside[11] thee............ daughter of............[12] of the town of........[13] (and by whatever other name or surname thou[14] and

[1] In those countries where divorce of Jewish couples is governed by the law of the land, it is considered necessary for them to go through the ceremony of a Jewish divorce, in addition to the ordinary legal procedure; likewise a religious marriage ceremony, *more judaico*, is usually performed after the civil marriage.
[2] Mishnah Gittin ix, 4; viii, 5; iii, 2.
[3] Id. viii, 5; Mishnah Yadayim iv, 8.
[4] Mishnah Gittin viii, 5.
[5] Id. ix, 5; iii, 2.
[6] Id. viii, 5.
[7] Id. ix, 8; Mishnah Yebamoth iii, 8.
[8] Mishnah Gittin viii, 5; iv, 2.
[9] Mishnah Yebamoth xiv, 1.
[10] Ibid.
[11] Mishnah Gittin ix, 3.
[12] Id. ix, 5; iii, 2.
[13] Id. viii, 5.
[14] Id. ix, 8.

thy father are known, and thy town and his town),[1] who hast been my wife from time past hitherto; and hereby I do release thee and send thee away and put thee aside[2] that thou mayest have permission and control over thyself to go to be married to any man whom thou desirest,[3] and no man shall hinder thee (in my name) from this day forever. And thou art permitted (to be married) to any man.[4] And these presents shall be unto thee from me a bill of dismissal, a document of release and a letter of freedom,[5] according to the law of Moses and Israel.

........the son of........a witness
........the son of........a witness."[6]

BLANK FORMS.—During the period of the Mishnah blank forms were used by the scribes or notaries in the preparation of all sorts of legal documents including bills of divorce. This custom was opposed by Rabbi Yehudah (150-210 C.E.), the compiler of the Mishnah, and by Rabbi Eliezer, on the ground that the laws of divorce must be strictly interpreted, and inasmuch as the law provides that the husband shall write *her* a bill of divorce, it is necessary that the document should be specially prepared at or immediately before the time when it is intended to be used as an instrument of divorce, and it is therefore unlawful to prepare a

[1] Mishnah Gittin viii, 5; iv, 2.
[2] Id. ix, 3.
[3] Ibid.
[4] Id. ix, 1, 3.
[5] Id. ix, 3.
[6] Id. ix, 4, 7, 8.

FORM OF BILL OF DIVORCE. 159

portion of the document beforehand when it is not yet known for whom it will be used.[1] In spite of these opinions, however, the use of blank forms was continued.

THE FOLDED GET.—A curious form of the Bill of Divorce was known as the Folded Get, which was prepared in the following manner:

Two or three lines were written, then the parchment was folded and fastened, so that the two lines written were entirely covered over, and a witness signed on the back of the fold; then two more lines were written, and again the parchment was folded and fastened, and this fold attested by another witness. So that it became a maxim that the folded Get must have as many witnesses as it has folds, and if one fold is blank, the Get was called a "bald Get," and was void.[2]

The reason and origin of this curious form seem to have been forgotten at a very early period, and the Talmudists exercised their ingenuity in inventing reasons to account for it.

One of the most plausible was that which received the sanction of two great Talmudical commentators, Rashi (1040-1105 C. E.) and Rabbi Obadiah, of Bartinora (1470-1520 C. E.). According to this view, the folded Get was invented to meet the case of priests who, in a fit of anger, divorced their wives; the cumbrous formality delayed and protracted the procedure, and thereby gave

[1] Mishnah Gittin iii, 2.
[2] Mishnah Gittin viii, 9, 10.

the parties an opportunity for reconciliation.[1] The priest could not, like the ordinary Israelite, remarry his divorced wife, for the Biblical law provided that a priest should not marry a divorced woman, and this provision was held to include his own divorced wife.[2]

Dr. J. M. Rabbinowicz suggests[3] that the folded Get probably was a Persian custom adopted by the Jews during the Captivity in Babylon. But there is some evidence in the Book of Jeremiah of an analogous custom well known and established in Judea. In his purchase of the field of Hanam'el, Jeremiah prepared two deeds, one of which was sealed, *i. e.*, rolled up, fastened and then sealed, and the other left open; the former to be referred to in case the latter had been lost or tampered with.[4] It is probable, therefore, that the sealed or folded Get was used both in Babylon and Judea, and that the difference in procedure between the execution of the deed of Jeremiah and the folding-up and attestation of the "Folded Get" was the result of time and local custom. It appears that there was some discussion whether a plain Get was valid if the witnesses signed on the back, and whether a folded Get was valid if the witnesses signed within. The patriarch Rabbi Simon ben Gamaliel[5] decided that this question depended on the custom of the

[1] Talmud Babli Baba Bathra 160 b.
[2] Leviticus xxi, 7.
[3] Rabbinowicz, "Legislation Civile du Thalmud," Vol. IV, p. 368.
[4] Jeremiah xxxii, 10-14
[5] Died about 170 C. E.

FORM OF BILL OF DIVORCE. 161

land, *i. e.*, the local custom and law of the country in which the Jews dwelt.¹

The essential features of the Get were the date, the names of the parties, proper words indicating the complete separation of the husband and wife, and the signatures of the witnesses. The language commonly used in Bills of Divorce was Aramaic, although the use of Hebrew, Greek or other languages was not uncommon.² It was improper, of course, to introduce irrelevant matter into the body of the Get,³ although alterations or interlineations could be made, and would not affect the validity of the instrument, if noted at the end and before the witnesses signed their names.⁴

DATE.—It was, at one time, the custom to date the Bill of Divorce from the reign of Alexander of Macedon; but as the scribes during the Middle Ages were not well versed in Greek chronology, it became the established custom to date the documents from the year of the creation of the world, according to the traditional calculation,⁵ and to add the date according to the era current in the place where it was written, out of respect for the secular authorities and " on account of the peace of the Government."⁶ It seems that in some instances

¹ Mishnah Baba Bathra x, 1. The term "Get" is here used in its simple sense of "document," including all written acts as well as Bills of Divorce.
² Mishnah Gittin ix, 8.
³ Talmud Babli Baba Bathra 176 a.
⁴ Maimonides' Treatise Gerushin iv, 15.
⁵ Hagaoth Maimuni to Gerushin i, 27.
⁶ Maimonides' Treatise Gerushin i, 27.

sentiment prompted the dating of Bills of Divorce according to the reign of extinct Median or Greek dynasties. These documents were held to be void, as they tended to irritate the public authorities and were subversive of the public peace.[1] For the same reason documents which were dated from the destruction of the Temple at Jerusalem were declared void, as tending no doubt to unduly exaggerate the strained relations between the Roman conquerors and the conquered Jews.[2]

Before the destruction of the Temple, while the religious conflicts between the Sadducees and Pharisees were raging, one of the Sadducees sarcastically charged the Pharisees with a lack of respect for the memory of the great Lawgiver, Moses, because they placed the name of the heathen sovereign and Moses in the same document; the former being introduced at the beginning of the document (in the date) and the latter in the very last phrase thereof. The Pharisees justified their custom by pointing out, with equal irony, that if it was an offense to couple the name of the heathen sovereign and Moses, then Moses himself was guilty of a greater offense in coupling the name of the Egyptian Pharaoh with the name of God, and even giving the former precedence, as it is written,[3] "And Pharaoh said, Who is the Lord that I should obey his voice?"[4]

[1] Mishnah Gittin viii, 8.
[2] Ibid.
[3] Exodus v, 2.
[4] Mishnah Yadayim iv, 8.

FORM OF BILL OF DIVORCE. 163

DIES JURIDICI.—A Get written on the Sabbath day[1] or on any of the festivals, or on the New Year's Day, or the Day of Atonement,[2] was void, if it was deliberately written in violation of the law,[3] but if the scribe did not know that it was the Sabbath or Holy day and innocently wrote the Get, it was valid.[4] These were *dies non juridici*, on which all work was strictly prohibited by law, the act of writing being especially mentioned as a species of work. Although the middle days of the Passover Festival and of the Festival of Tabernacles, called Hol Hammoéd, were also *dies non juridici*, Bills of Divorce could be written on these days.[5]

In cases where the date was omitted, a presumption arose against the validity of the Get, and shifted the burden of proof on the wife.[6] In strict

[1] Mishnah Shabbath xii, 3.
[2] Mishnah Moëd Qaton iii, 6. Also Mishnah Meghillah, i, 5.
[3] Maimonides' Treatise Gerushin iii, 19.
[4] Ibid.
[5] Talmud Yerushalmi Moëd Qaton sub Mishnah iii, 3 (82 a). On the "middle days" most of the ordinary affairs of life were conducted and all works necessary to the public welfare were attended to (Mishnah Moëd Qaton i, 2). Marriages were not allowed to take place during the Moëd, and the reason given therefore was, that the individual joy of the married man would interfere with his duty to participate in the general joy of the festival. In connection with the law allowing women to prepare their ornaments on the Moëd, it is interesting to note this little touch. Rabbi Juda said: "The woman must not apply paste to her face during the Moëd, because it temporarily disfigures her." (Mishnah Moëd Qaton i, 7.)
[6] Mishnah Gittin ix, 4.

law, the writing and attestation of the Get had to take place on the same day.[1] The legal day of the Hebrews began and ended at sunset. It was considered necessary that a legal act once begun should be completed on the same day, except in the trial of criminal cases, in which the contrary rule obtained.

NAMES.—Rabban Gamaliel the Elder (about 40 C. E.) ordained that after the name and place of residence of both parties the following phrase should be added : "And by what other name he or she may be known."[2] It was customary to write in the Get the name by which the parties were best known, and even in cases where merely a nickname was written, it was declared to be valid, provided the person was well known by such name.[3]

WORDS OF SEPARATION.—The essential words of the Get indicating the absolute separation of the husband and wife were, " Thou art permitted unto any man," or, according to Rabbi Yehudah, " Thou hast herewith from me a bill of dismissal, a document of release and a letter of freedom, that thou mayst go and be married to any man thou mayst like." [4]

CLAUSES IN RESTRAINT OF MARRIAGE.—Any attempt made by the husband to restrain the divorced wife from freely entering into marriage with any one whom she pleased rendered the Get

[1] Mishnah Gittin ii, 2.
[2] Id. iv, 2.
[3] Id. ix, 8.
[4] Mishnah Gittin ix, 3.

FORM OF BILL OF DIVORCE. 165

null and void; the divorce was absolutely *a vinculo matrimonii*, and the wife had an unconditional right to enter into a second marriage. Rabbi Eliezer seemed to have been the only one of the prominent Doctors of the law to maintain that the husband could control the action of the wife after she was divorced. He held a Get valid which declared "Thou art free to marry any man except A. B." But the opinion of all of the other sages was against it.[1] If the restriction extended only to persons whom the wife could not legally marry, as, for instance, if the husband wrote in the Get, "Thou mayst marry any one except thy father, or a slave," etc., it was treated as surplusage, and did not affect the validity of the Get.[2] But if the restriction sought to prevent marriage with one whose marriage with the divorced woman was not void, although not favored by the law, as, for instance, the marriage of the divorced woman to a priest,[3] the Get was a nullity.[4]

DIVORCES COUPLED WITH CONDITIONS.—The husband had not only the right to divorce his wife, but he could couple the divorce with conditions, upon the fulfilment of which its validity depended.

Nothing will illustrate more clearly the true theory of the ancient law as to the position of the husband than this right to couple the divorce with conditions. The constitution of the patriarchal

[1] Mishnah Gittin ix, 1.
[2] Id. ix, 2.
[3] Leviticus xxi, 7.
[4] Mishnah Gittin ix, 2.

family left the husband supreme in the household; he had absolute power and control over the members of his little kingdom, and also could release them from his sovereignty. He could manumit his slave and divorce his wife whenever it pleased him; and that he could exact the performance of some act by them as a condition precedent to their release from his power, is an inference that requires no demonstration. Herein, therefore, is to be found the origin of the custom respecting conditions attached to divorces. Upon this ancient theory of the law, based upon immemorial practice, and arising out of the conditions of the patriarchal household, the entire later system of law governing the domestic relations was established. Unless this theory be kept in view constantly, the study of the Jewish law of husband and wife, parent and child, and master and slave, will present a chaos of rules and decisions without coherence or system. By means of this theory, a synthetic study of the law will bring all of the rules, opinions and decisions into harmony and correlation.

The conditions that could be attached to the divorce depended entirely upon the caprice of the husband. Originally it is likely that the husband could put away his wife and at the same time forbid her to marry another, and thus *taboo* her to all the world. There is no evidence that such actually was the condition at any period within historical time in the Jewish domestic law. But it is a fair inference, from our knowledge of the power of the patriarch over his family and household. It was shown above,[1] that an attempt by the husband to restrain the wife from entering into the marriage state with another was declared unlawful by the Tanaïm. This certainly shows that it must have been practised and considered lawful before it was legally interdicted. And this seems to be the only case in which the Rabbis declared a condition annexed to the Get void. A second step forward was made when the Rabbis declared that it lay in the power of the woman to accept or reject the Get, whenever the condition attached to it was the performance of some act by her. If the husband annexed a condition to the divorce providing that it should not become absolute unless his wife paid him two hundred pieces of money and the woman accepted the Get, she became liable for the payment of the amount named; but if she refused to fulfil the condition she was not divorced.[2]

This privilege, to fulfil the condition if she pleased, or to refuse to do so, was, in all cases where the Get had conditions annexed, tantamount to giving the woman the right to determine whether or not she would be divorced. If there was no condition attached to the Get, she was, under the old law, divorced *nolens volens*.

The general rule required that conditions be strictly fulfilled. Where the husband provided that the wife should pay him a sum of money within a certain period, in default of which pay-

[1] Supra, p. 164.
[2] Maimonides' Treatise Ishuth vi, 18.

ment the Get should be declared void, payment after the expiration of the time was too late.[1] Rabbi Simon ben Gamaliel seems to have been inclined to interpret the conditions attached to a Get in favor of the wife. In one case, at Sidon, the condition was that the wife should give her husband a certain cloak, for which he seemed to have a special desire. The woman lost the cloak, and it was held that she could fulfil the condition by giving him its equivalent in money.[2] It was contended that if the condition annexed to the Get was, that the wife should serve her husband's father for two years, and if the father died before the expiration of the two years, the divorce was null and void, because the condition was not strictly fulfilled, the woman not having served for two years. But Rabbi Simon ben Gamaliel was of the opinion that the impossibility of fulfilling the condition was not her fault, but was an act of God, and that therefore the divorce was valid.[3]

DIVORCE ON CONDITION OF THE HUSBAND'S FAILURE TO RETURN.—Another form of the divorce on condition provided that the divorce should become absolute in case the absent husband did not return within a definite period, and if he died while abroad during this time, the wife was divorced. The use of this form arose in cases where the husband went abroad or to sea, or on a journey with a caravan through the desert. As

[1] Mishnah Gittin vii, 5.
[2] Ibid.
[3] Mishnah Gittin vii, 6.

the absence of the husband raised no legal presumption of death, his widow could never remarry if he died while abroad, and no legal proof of his death could be found. This case was met by a Get on condition.[1] If he returned before the time had elapsed, this was equivalent to a reconciliation, and the Get was void; but after the time had elapsed, the Get became absolute and the woman was free.

It was decided in a case where the husband going abroad left an order for a Get to be written and delivered to his wife, on condition of his absence for more than twelve months, that the Get must be written and delivered to the wife after the period specified, and that if it is written before the expiration of the time and delivered to her it is void, because the condition was not absolutely fulfilled.

DIVORCE ON CONDITION OF THE HUSBAND'S DEATH.—The husband could make his own death the condition upon which the divorce became valid;[2] the happening of this event worked retroactively, and during the interval between the delivery of the Get and his death, the wife was, according to Rabbi Yehudah, considered a married woman in every respect, but, according to Rabbi Yosé, one whose divorce is doubtful.[3] This peculiar use of the Get on Condition seems likely to have arisen out of the desire of the husband to save his wife from the Levirate marriage.[4]

[1] Mishnah Gittin vii, 8.
[2] Id. 3.
[3] Mishnah Gittin vii, 4.
[4] Talmud Babli Nedarim 27 a (Rashi).

According to the law, the death of the husband without issue made his wife *ipso facto* the bride of his brother, whose duty it was to marry her, or release her through the ceremony of Haliça.[1] The divorced woman was of course not subject to this law. Where the brother-in-law was distasteful to the husband or the wife, it would be quite natural to make use of the Get on Condition, in order to prevent him from having any claim upon the wife after her husband's death. So that when the husband gave his wife a Bill of Divorce, on condition that it should become absolute at his death, she remained his wife as long as he lived; but at the moment of his death she was not his widow, but a divorced woman.[2]

[1] Deuteronomy xxv, 5-10.
[2] Mishnah Gittin vii, 3. There was a tradition cited by Rabbi Samuel bar Nahmani that the warriors of King David, on going to war, gave bills of divorce to their wives to take effect in case they died in battle (Talmud Babli Kethuboth 9 b), supra, p. 134.

CHAPTER XIV.

ATTESTATION AND DELIVERY OF THE BILL OF DIVORCE (GET).

The Get was Attested by Two Witnesses—Who were Personally Acquainted with the Husband and Wife—The Delivery of the Get was Essential to Complete the Divorce—Method of Delivery—Delivery to Minor Wife—Delivery by Messenger—Presumption that the Husband is Alive at the Time the Messenger delivers the Get—Who may be Messenger—The Messengers of the Husband—The Messengers of the Wife—Sub-Messengers.

THE ATTESTATION OF THE GET.—The Get having been written was not signed by the husband, his name appearing in the body thereof, but was attested by the signatures of two competent witnesses, who were not related to the parties and were not otherwise legally disqualified.[1] These wrote their prænomen and patronymic followed by the word 'Ed (a witness), thus:
"Reuben ben (son of) Jacob, 'Ed."[2]
The names could be signed in any language.[3]

Although it was not absolutely essential that there should be subscribing witnesses to the Get, Rabban Gamaliel ordained on account of public

[1] Mishnah Sanhedrin iii, 3.
[2] Mishnah Gittin ix, 4.
[3] Id. ix, 8.

policy, that in order to facilitate the proof of legal documents the witnesses should subscribe.[1] Their attestation raised a presumption in favor of the validity of the document, and the burden of proving the contrary was upon him who attacked it.

After this ordinance requiring the attestation of witnesses to the document, it was still for a long time maintained that the Get could be otherwise proved, and Rabbi Eliezer (about 150 C. E.) held that in a case where there were no subscribing witnesses, but where the Get had been properly delivered to the wife, in the presence of witnesses, it was valid and could be proved by the witnesses of the delivery.[2] This decision was rendered after the rebellion of Bar Kokhba, when the danger attending the preparation and delivery of a Bill of Divorce was very great, the death penalty having been decreed against all persons indulging in this practice; hence exact conformity with the prescribed regulations was often impossible.[3]

In strict law, it was essential that the witnesses should be personally acquainted with the husband and wife, so that they might literally be said to know that this particular Bill of Divorce was written and intended for a certain woman.[4] This being premised, the Get could be prepared in the absence of the woman, whose identity could afterwards be established by the witnesses.[5]

[1] Mishnah Gittin iv, 3.
[2] Id. ix, 4.
[3] Talmud Babli Gittin 64 a.
[4] Mishnah Gittin iii, 1.
[5] Mishnah Baba Bathra x, 4.

ATTESTATION AND DELIVERY OF THE GET. 173

But cases sometimes arose where the exigencies of the situation demanded that legal acts should be done without the usual formalities; as, for instance, where the husband was in danger of his life and ordered a Bill of Divorce for his wife, it was decided in the College of Rabbi Ishmael that the Bill of Divorce might be written and delivered to her even though the witnesses did not personally know the parties.[1]

As stated above, the witnesses signed their prænomen and patronymic, and added the word "a witness." If, however, the name was only partially written it was nevertheless a valid attestation, or if the word "a witness" was omitted, it was nevertheless presumed that the subscriber wrote his name with the intention of being a witness to the document. As, for instance:

"Reuben............a witness."
Or,
"............the son of Jacob, a witness."
Or,
"Reuben the son of Jacob............"[2]

[1] Talmud Babli Gittin 66 a.
[2] Mishnah Gittin ix, 8. The Mishnah states that it was the custom of some of the best men in Jerusalem to attest documents in this way, not writing the word "'Ed" after their names; and the Gemara cites a number of instances of distinguished judges who used marks or seals. For instance, Abba Areka, commonly called Rab (*The Master*, 175-247 C. E.), the greatest of all the Jewish Doctors of the law in Babylonia, in attesting documents made a mark in the shape of a fish. Rabbi Ḥanina's mark was a branch of a date palm. Rabbi Ḥasda used the second letter of his name, "Samekh" ("S"), and Raba Bar Rab Huna used as a seal

THE DELIVERY OF THE GET.—The final step in the divorce procedure was the delivery of the Bill of Divorce to the wife. This was ordinarily done by handing it to her with some words indicating that the document presented was a Bill of Divorce. In order to avoid doubt and to facilitate proof of divorce, it was ordained that the delivery of the Get should always be made in the presence of two witnesses,[1] who were otherwise competent to testify at Jewish law.[2] These witnessess at delivery were not absolutely essential, and if the Bill of Divorce had been delivered without witnesses, it was, nevertheless, presumed to have been properly delivered if it was found in the wife's possession, and its writing was proven by the subscribing witnesses.[3]

At the time of the delivery of the Get, the wife must have actual or presumptive notice of its nature and content. If the husband, after a conversation with his wife about their divorce, handed her a Bill of Divorce, she was presumed to know its nature from the previous conversation;[4] but if there had been no previous conversation about it, it was necessary for the husband to give his wife formal notice that the document handed to her

the emblem of a mast of a ship (Talmud Babli Baba Bathra 161 b; Talmud Yerushalmi Gittin sub Mishnah ix, 8; Talmud Babli Gittin 36 a). It is the custom of modern judges to attest certain documents, especially orders of court, by their initials instead of writing out their names in full.

[1] Mishnah Gittin ix, 4.
[2] Talmud Babli Qiddushin 43 a.
[3] Maimonides' Gerushin i, 16.
[4] Mishnah Maaser Shēni iv, 7.

ATTESTATION AND DELIVERY OF THE GET. 175

was a Bill of Divorce.[1] Hence, if the husband handed the Get to his wife, telling her that it is a bond or some other document, or if he put it into her lap while she was asleep, she was not divorced.[2]

As soon as the Get came into possession of the wife she was divorced. It was not necessary that she should have actual manual seizure of it; but if it was brought under her control or within her reach, or placed in the hand of her authorized agent, she was divorced. Therefore, if the husband threw the Get towards her while she was in her own house or in her own courtyard, it was considered a valid delivery, because the Get was then in her possession.[3] But if he cast it towards her in his own house, it was not a valid delivery,[4] unless it actually came into her own hand, because being in his own house he is supposed by a legal presumption to retain possession of the document. If he cast it towards her on neutral ground, or on the public highway, she was divorced if it fell nearer to her than to him, being then considered to be in her possession.[5]

A curious case of mistake in the delivery of the Get is cited in the Mishnah. The scribe prepared two documents, a Get for the wife and an acknowledgment of receipt of the amount of the Kethubah for the husband. By mistake, he handed the Get to the wife and the receipt to the

[1] Talmud Babli Qiddushin 6 a.
[2] Mishnah Gittin viii, 2.
[3] Mishnah Gittin viii, 1.
[4] Ibid.
[5] Id. viii, 2.

husband. They, being illiterate, exchanged the documents, the husband thinking that he was delivering the Get to the wife and the wife thinking that she was giving the receipt to the husband. Afterwards the mistake was discovered. In the meantime, the woman had remarried, and it was contended that her second marriage was void and that therefore she could not live either with her first or her second husband. But Rabbi Eliezer was of the opinion, which was accepted as a correct statement of the law, that if the mistake had been discovered before her second marriage, the divorce would have been declared void, and the husband could have given her a second Get, or could have become reconciled to her. But having entered into a second marriage and having acquired a new status, the mere mistake in the exchange of the documents would not be permitted to affect or disturb it.[1]

DELIVERY OF THE GET TO A MINOR WIFE.—Where a minor had been betrothed, and her affianced husband desired to release her, he had to give her a Bill of Divorce, as though they had been actually married, and this Get had to be delivered to her father and not to her.[2] But after the minor has been married, her father's guardianship over her is absolutely at an end, and hence it seems that she would be entitled to receive the Get herself.[3] If, however, the minor was so young as not to understand the nature of a Get, she could

---

[1] Mishnah Gittin viii, 8.
[2] Mishnah Kethuboth iv, 4.
[3] Talmud Yerushalmi Gittin vi, sub Mishnah ii. See Rashi to Talmud Babli Qiddushin 43 b, sub Tit. " Hi ve'abiha."

not be divorced at all.[1] As long as the minor was merely betrothed, her father could appoint a messenger to receive her Get, but after she was married, she could be divorced only by actual delivery of the Get to her; for a minor could not appoint an agent or messenger or attorney.[2]

THE DELIVERY OF THE GET BY A MESSENGER. —The Biblical law provides that the husband shall give the wife a bill of divorce. Upon the well-known doctrine that the act of an agent is the act of the principal, the Mishnah provides that both the husband and wife, living apart, could appoint lawful agents or messengers to give and receive the bill of divorce.

The doctrine of agency was well known, especially through the Roman law, but the Rabbis sought some Biblical foundation for it. Rabbi Joshua ben Qorḥa sought to prove this doctrine by the following text:[3] "And the whole assembly of the Congregation of Israel shall kill it (the Paschal lamb) at evening." "Here," said the Rabbi, "is a case where it is physically impossible to carry out the letter of the law; the meaning must be that one kills the lamb for all the participants, and his act is considered the act of his constituency."[4]

PRESUMPTION OF LIFE.—The authority of the messenger to deliver the Get was revoked by the death of the husband.

[1] Mishnah Gittin vi, 2.
[2] Id. vi, 3.
[3] Exodus xii, 6.
[4] Talmud Babli Qiddushin 41 b.

In order to avoid vexatious litigation to determine whether a man was yet alive at the time the Get was delivered, it was laid down as a general rule that in all cases the husband, who was alive when the messenger started on his journey, was presumed to be alive when the Get was delivered to the wife; even where the husband was sick or very aged, he was presumed to be alive at the time when his messenger delivered the Get.[1] This was an important presumption of law, inasmuch as there could be no divorce after the death of the husband;[2] and if the Get was invalid, the wife became a widow and not a divorced woman, whereby her status was materially changed.

According to the decision of Rabbi Eliezer ben Parta, when a man charged with a capital crime was being led to *trial* for his life, he was presumed to be alive at a subsequent time (when a legal act was performed which required his existence to give it validity); but if he was being led to *execution*, the fact of his existence becomes a question to be determined by proof. Hence, if a man while being tried for his life, sent a letter of divorce to his wife, he was presumed to be still alive when it was delivered to her; but if he was being led to execution, this presumption did not arise. Rabbi Joseph was of the opinion that if a man was being led to execution in obedience to the sentence of a Jewish Court, the presumption is in favor of life, for the Jewish law gives him the benefit of the slightest

[1] Mishnah Gittin iii, 3.
[2] Ibid. i, 6.

particle of evidence, in order to stay the execution and allow a new trial; but if the sentence was imposed by a Court of the Gentiles (Romans), he is presumed to have been executed; for "when a man is condemned by them he will surely be put to death."[1]

WHO MAY BE A MESSENGER.—All persons are competent to act as messengers for the husband or the wife, except deaf-mutes and idiots, because they are *non compotes;* infants, because of their non-age; blind persons, because they cannot see from whom the Get is brought or to whom it is delivered, and therefore their testimony in doubtful cases would be of little value; heathen and slaves, because they are not within the pale of the Jewish law, which looks upon divorce as a religious act.[2] All other persons are competent, even those who in ordinary legal proceedings would be deemed incompetent. The danger of fraud or perjury is to a large extent obviated by the document, which, having been properly written and attested, proves itself.[3]

The messenger must strictly follow the instructions of his principal and any act contrary to such instructions is void.[4] But if the instructions given to the messenger are general, he may, within a certain scope, evercise his discretion in the performance of his duty. If, for example, the mes-

[1] Talmud Babli Gittin 28 b.
[2] Mishnah Gittin ii, 5; Talmud Babli Gittin 23 b.
[3] Mishnah Gittin ii, 7; Mishnah Yebamoth xv, 4.
[4] Mishnah Gittin vi, 3.

senger is told to deliver the Get at a particular place, he has no power to deliver it elsewhere. But if it is merely suggested to him that he may find the wife at a particular place for the purpose of delivering the Get to her, he may, if he does not find her there, deliver the Get to her elsewhere.[1]

The law recognized five classes of agents or messengers, two of them being the appointees of the husband, two of the wife and the fifth being the appointee of the messenger or of the court, to act as a substitute for the one originally appointed. These five classes of messengers may be considered under the following heads :

First, the messenger for the delivery of the Get; second, the messenger for the delivery of the Get from foreign parts; third, the messenger for bringing the Get to the wife; fourth, the messenger for receiving the Get for the wife; and fifth, sub-messengers.

THE MESSENGER FOR DELIVERY.—The messenger of the husband, appointed to deliver the Get, stands in the place of his principal. In the eye of the law his act is the act of the husband who appointed him, and when he delivers the Get it is supposed to be the act of the husband himself, unless positive proof is adduced that he has exceeded the authority conferred upon him.

THE MESSENGER FROM FOREIGN PARTS.—The messenger who brought a Get from the husband to the wife within the boundaries of Palestine, need not have been a witness of the writing and the

[1] Mishnah Gittin vi, 3.

attestation, since any question as to the proper preparation and execution of the Get could be settled by the testimony of the subscribing witnesses.[1] But when the messenger brought the Get from a foreign country into Palestine, or vice versa, or from one province or jurisdiction into another, when both are situated beyond the boundaries of Palestine, or from one hostile jurisdiction into another within Palestine, it was necessary that he should have witnessed the writing and attestation of the Get, so that he could, when delivering it, testify "before me it was written and before me it was subscribed."[2]

This statement of the messenger raised a strong presumption in favor of the validity of the Get. The scribe who wrote it was presumed to have been "scrupulously exact"[3] in the performance of his duty, and this presumption, together with the presumption of the moral responsibility of the messenger,[4] were deemed equivalent to the testimony of two witnesses; the strict rules of evidence were relaxed in this case, lest the wife become an Egunah.

If, therefore, the messenger could not testify that it was written and subscribed in his presence, the Get was void,[5] unless the subscribing witnesses were produced to authenticate it;[6] it being consid-

[1] Mishnah Gittin i, 3.
[2] Id. i, 1.
[3] Talmud Babli Gittin 2 b.
[4] Id. 3 a.
[5] Mishnah Gittin ii, 1.
[6] Id. i, 3.

ered less dangerous to declare the Get void than to allow the wife to remarry on the faith of it and afterwards subject her to the necessity of proving that she had been divorced, in a case where the divorce had been sent to her from a distant land, and the difficulties of proving her position would be almost insurmountable.[1]

THE MESSENGER FOR BRINGING THE GET TO THE WIFE.—The wife may appoint a messenger to bring the Get to her from the husband or his messenger, but her messenger is not deemed to be absolutely her representative, unless he is appointed by a special formality, and she is not divorced until he has actually delivered the Get into her hands.[2] This principle is illustrated in the case of the wife of a priest. As his wife, she was entitled to share in the votive offerings that were set aside for the sustenance of the priest and his family. After she had appointed a messenger to bring the Get from her husband, the question arose whether she was still entitled to the above rights, and it was decided that she was not divorced, and, therefore, not deprived of her rights until the Get was actually delivered into her hands.[3]

THE MESSENGER FOR RECEIVING THE GET FOR THE WIFE.—It is, of course, presumed that the appointment of any of the three former classes of messengers is made in the presence of witnesses, but in the case of the appointment by the

[1] Maimonides' Treatise Gerushin vii, 8.
[2] Mishnah Gittin vi, 4.
[3] Ibid.

wife of a messenger to receive her Get, the law provides that the presence of two sets of witnesses is required, one pair or set to prove the appointment of the messenger and the other pair to prove the reception of the Get by him.[1] Thereby this messenger becomes her lawful representative, and the delivery of the Get to him has the same effect as the delivery to her, and she is divorced as soon as the Get reaches his hands.[2]

As stated above, she must have two witnesses to testify that she appointed him her messenger, and two witnesses (although these may be the same persons as the witnesses of the appointment) to testify that the Get was delivered to the messenger and *that he tore it up*.[3]

The tearing up of the Get is said, by Rabbi Yehudah, to refer to the period of public danger, when Bills of Divorce were classed among the numerous religious and quasi-religious acts which the Roman authorities interdicted.[4] The period referred to is the one following the rebellion of the Jews under Bar Kokhba, during the reign of Hadrian.[5] In order to avoid detection, it became customary to destroy the Get immediately after it was delivered, and this, of course, had to be done in the presence of witnesses, in order to perpetuate the proof of delivery in the absence of the Bill of Divorce.

[1] Mishnah Gittin vi, 2.
[2] Talmud Babli Gittin 64 a; Maimonides' Gerushin vi, 1
[3] Mishnah Gittin vi, 2.
[4] Talmud Babli Gittin 64 a.
[5] Graetz's " History of the Jews," Vol. II, p. 422.

SUB-MESSENGERS. — Although ordinarily the maxim *delegatus non potest delegare* obtained, there were some cases in which the strictness of the law yielded to the exigencies of the situation; as, for instance, when a messenger carrying a Get from one place to another, in Palestine, fell sick while on the road, he could constitute a sub-messenger to deliver the Get for him.[1] If, however, in addition to his appointment by the husband to deliver the Get, he had been commissioned to receive from the wife, at the time when he delivered the Get to her, some article of value, for the purpose of bringing it back to the husband, he could not delegate his authority,[2] because special trust and confidence had been reposed in him, and he became a bailee for the husband; and the bailee could not transfer the bailment to a third person without the consent of the owner.[3]

Where the messenger bringing a Get from foreign parts fell sick, or was for other reasons unable to continue his journey, he could not constitute a sub-messenger; for the messenger bringing the divorce from foreign parts had a special duty to perform at the time of the delivery of the Get, namely, to testify that it was written and attested in his presence; and the performance of this special duty could not be delegated to another. He was obliged to go before a Beth Din, or Court of Three, and make his deposition that the Get was

[1] Mishnah Gittin iii, 5.
[2] Ibid.
Maimonides' Treatise Sha'alah Uphiqadon iv. 8.

written and attested in his presence, and the Beth Din then appointed a messenger to deliver it. The substituted messenger, acting under the authority of the Beth Din, was merely obliged to announce himself as the messenger of the Court, instead of repeating the customary formula, "Before me it was written and before me it was subscribed."[1]

[1] Mishnah Gittin iii, 6.

CHAPTER XV.

WHEN THE GET IS NULL AND VOID, OR LOST.

The Husband's Right to Annul the Get Denied by Rabban Gamaliel—Attempts by Common Barrators to Cast Doubt on Divorce Proceeding—Ban of Excommunication—Proof of Divorce when Get is Lost—Uncorroborated Statement of the Divorced Wife.

ANNULLING THE GET.—Anciently, the husband could recall and annul the Get sent to his wife, before it had actually been delivered to her[1] or to her messenger appointed to receive it,[2] and in the same manner the master could annul the bill of manumission sent to his slave.[3]

In the year 40 of the present era, Rabban Gamaliel the Elder decreed that the husband could no longer annul his Bill of Divorce, except in the presence of the messenger or the wife.[4] And the Doctors of the law decided that although the bill of divorce might be annulled in this manner, the bill of manumission, having been written and given to the messenger, could never be annulled by the master. An old maxim of the law was here applied. According to it, an advantage could be conferred

[1] Mishnah Gittin iv, 2.
[2] Id. vi, 1.
[3] Id. i, 6.
[4] Id. iv, 2.

(186)

upon a person in his absence, but nothing could be done in derogation of his rights except in his presence. The Bill of Divorce could be revoked and annulled, because such revocation and annulment was an advantage to the wife; but the Bill of Manumission of the slave could not be annulled, because such annulment would be decidedly to his disadvantage.[1] Here may be seen the parting of the ways in the law referring to the status of the wife and the slave. There is no longer merely a consideration for the right of the husband and master, but the right of the wife and the bondsman are carefully protected. It is considered that it is better for the woman to be married than to be free, *i. e.* divorced, but that it is better for the slave to be free than to be under the power of the master.

After the Get had been delivered, the woman was divorced and was free to marry again after three months.[2] The divorce was absolute and it was beyond the power of the husband to annul the Get; but it sometimes happened that common barrators sought to annoy the divorced couple and extort money by raising questions as to the legality of the divorce.

In order to prevent this, a Sanhedrin which met at Troyes (about 1150 C. E.) decreed the ban of excommunication against any person who attempted to criticise the procedure for the purpose of casting doubt upon the legality of the divorce.[3]

[1] Mishnah Gittin i, 6.
[2] Supra, p. 108.
[3] Eben Haëzer cliv, 22, Graetz's "History of the Jews," Vol. VI, p. 200.

188 THE JEWISH LAW OF DIVORCE.

PROOF OF DIVORCE WHERE THE GET OR THE WITNESSES CANNOT BE PRODUCED.—As was shown above,[1] the proof of the divorce is the production of the Get in the possession of the wife, and where there is any doubt as to its validity, or where it has been lost or destroyed, it may be proved by testimony of the subscribing witnessses or of the witnesses present at its delivery to the wife. But cases may arise in which it is impossible either to produce the Get or to call the witnesses to establish it. In such cases, if no exception were made to the rules of law as to proof of the divorce, the woman would practically remain a married woman forever. But the Mishnah provides that in such cases the mere uncorroborated statement of the woman may be accepted as evidence of her divorce, provided there be no positive testimony of her marriage. If the woman stated that she had been married and was thereafter divorced, in the absence of all positive evidence, her statement is taken to be true upon the principle that "the mouth which binds may unbind," and she may be declared free to enter into a second matrimonial alliance.[2] For, if the woman had not stated that she was married, it would not have been necessary for her to state that she was divorced, and in the absence of all evidence she would have been presumed to be unmarried, and could have entered into marriage without being obliged to justify herself. It is therefore reasonable and

[1] Supra, p. 105.
[2] Mishnah Kethuboth ii, 5.

proper that where she had bound herself by her statement that she was married, she should be allowed to free herself by her statement that she was divorced. But if there is positive testimony that she is a married woman, her mere statement to the contrary is not sufficient to free her. If, however, the woman made her statement before the Beth Din, and was authorized to remarry, and after her second marriage witnesses appeared and testified that she was a married woman, their testimony would not annul the second marriage.[1]

In a case decided by Rabbi Yoḥanan of Tiberias (born 199, died 279 C.E.), it was held that even though the woman had not yet remarried, the decision of the Court, authorizing her to do so, would not be affected by the subsequent testimony of witnesses as to her first marriage.[2]

Similarly, if the woman is a minor, and her father makes a statement to the effect that he had given her in marriage and had afterwards received her divorce during her minority, she is to be treated as a divorced woman.[3] For during the minority of the woman, the father alone had the right to give her in marriage or to receive her Get; and his statement had the like effect and was governed by the same principles as the statement of the woman herself, when she has attained her majority; after she has attained her majority

[1] Mishnah Kethuboth ii, 5.
[2] Talmud Yerushalmi Kethuboth ii, sub Mishnah v (26 c).
[3] Mishnah Qiddushin iii, 8.

the statement made by her father was of no effect, inasmuch as she was no longer in his *manus*.[1]

If there was a rumor in town that a woman was betrothed, she could not marry unless this rumor was disproved. But if this rumor was followed by another that she had been divorced, she was to be so considered; for "the rumor which binds may unbind," in the absence of positive testimony.[2]

It may be taken as a general rule that in all cases where there was no positive evidence, the uncorroborated statement of the woman was sufficient to establish her status, namely, to determine whether she was married or unmarried, a divorced woman or a widow.[3]

It must be remembered that in the early stages of the law, the woman was hardly considered a legal person at all and, therefore, even so obvious a principle that, in the absence of direct testimony, the woman's own statement would be sufficient to establish her status, was not recognized; and it should, therefore, not be a matter of surprise to find this principle stated in the Mishnah and expressed

---

[1] Mishnah Qiddushin iii, 8.
[2] Mishnah Gittin ix, 9.
[3] In the case of Ganer *vs.* Lady Lanesborough, Peake's Nisi Prius Cases 17, (1791) before Lord Kenyon, a Jewess divorced at Leghorn. was permitted to prove her divorce *more judaico*. The document under the seal of the synagogue had been offered in evidence, and was held to be no proof, as the Court could not take judicial notice of the foreign law under which it had been executed. The divorced wife was then called to testify to the nature of the proceeding at Jewish law, and established the validity of her own divorce.

in the Gemara, for it was then an innovation and a departure from ancient custom; although to us, the principle involved seems almost axiomatic.

There was a case in which this principle was judicially announced. A beautiful woman had many suitors for her hand, and she invariably stated to all of them that she was a married woman. Some time thereafter, she accepted a suitor and married him. Inasmuch as she had upon her own testimony made a second marriage unlawful, she was brought before Rabbi Aḥa, and on being examined she said that she had merely made the statement for the purpose of getting rid of her objectionable suitors. Rabbi Aḥa referred the case to the Rabbinical College at Usha, and they declared that, inasmuch as the woman had assigned a good reason for her former statement, her testimony must be accepted as fact.[1]

[1] Talmud Babli Kethuboth 22 a.

CHAPTER XVI.

SEDER HA-GET.

Rules of Procedure in Divorce, as reported by Rabbi Joseph Karo in the Shulḥan Arukh, Treatise Eben Haëzer, Section 154, with occasional notes by Rabbi Moses Isserles.

NOTE.—During the days of the Talmudists, it was the custom to have a man learned in the law preside over the divorce proceeding, and the early Rabbis were accustomed to have the divorce procedure conducted only before the ablest authorities. It is therefore improper for any person to interfere in these matters unless he is learned in the law of marriage and divorce, and if such a one should endeavor, without being authorized, to conduct divorce proceedings, I am of the opinion that his acts should be declared null and void.

(1) It is the custom in some places not to conduct divorce proceedings on the eve of the Sabbath.

(2) A scribe and two witnesses must be present, none of whom is related to the other, nor to the husband or the wife.

NOTE.—The witnesses should be cautioned by the presiding Rabbi to review their lives and repent of any sin that they may have committed, lest through their sinfulness they should be incompetent to act in this proceeding. They should be men of understanding, who appreciate the meaning of divorce proceedings and, if they cannot read, the entire proceedings should be thoroughly explained to them beforehand.

(192)

(3) The scribe should not be one of the witnesses.

(4) The fee of the scribe and of the presiding Rabbi should not be greater than the value of their time.

NOTE.—The services of the one who presides are not like the services of a Judge, because his duties are merely ministerial. A Judge is not permitted to accept any fee for his judicial services.

(5) It is necessary that they should know the man to be the husband and the woman to be his wife; except in a period of public danger.

(6) If there should happen to be in the same city one whose name and that of his wife are identical with the names of the parties about to be divorced, the proceedings should not be conducted except in his presence.

(7) If the husband is sick, care should be taken to see that he is of sound mind at the time of the writing and delivery of the Get.

(8) If he desires to couple the divorce with a condition, it should not be mentioned to the scribe or to the subscribing witnesses until the document is delivered.

(9) All persons may write the bill of divorce except a deaf-mute, an idiot, a slave, an idolator, an Israelite who has apostatized, or one who willfully and maliciously breaks the Sabbath.

(10) The husband himself should not write the Get, unless no other person can be obtained to write it.

(11) In a like manner the husband should not

interfere with the scribe by directing him how to write the Get.

(12) If possible to obtain any other person no relative of the husband or of the wife should act as scribe.

(13) The scribe should furnish the parchment, ink and pen and all other material, and the husband should take possession of them by purchase.

(14) The Rabbi should ask the husband, "Do you give this Get of your own free will, without any compulsion ? If you have made any vow or taken any oath which binds you to give this Get, tell it to us and we will absolve you from its obligation." The husband should answer, "I have neither vowed nor sworn and I am under no compulsion, but I give this Get of my own free will without any compulsion or condition." If the husband should acknowledge that he has in any way bound himself to give the Get, he must first be absolved in order that he may act without compulsion. If he has given security that he will divorce his wife, it is not considered equivalent to the above cases, and he is not deemed then to be under restraint or compulsion in the sense above indicated.

(15) The husband hands the parchment and the pen and ink to the scribe in the presence of the witnesses, saying to him "Write for me a bill of divorce for my wife........the daughter of .... and for the purpose of separation, and I authorize you to write as many bills as may be necessary until one shall be produced which shall be without

flaw both in the writing and in the attestation, in accordance with the opinion of Rabbi ...."

(16) "And you .... and .... be witnesses and attest this Get for my wife .... the daughter of .... and for the purpose of separation and I authorize you to attest as many bills as may be necessary until one shall be produced which shall be without flaw both in the writing and in the attestation, in accordance with the opinion of Rabbi ...."

(17) If it be found necessary to write two bills of divorce on account of the doubt as to the proper names of the parties, the scribe and the witnesses should be specially authorized to do so.

(18) The scribe should not write and the witnesses should not sign until they have received the order from the mouth of the husband himself.

(19) The husband should pay the fee of the scribe. If he does not, the wife may pay it.

(20) The husband should state before the witnesses that he has not raised and will not raise any protest or declaration annulling the Get, and that anything which he had said or may say for this purpose shall be null and void, and that any witness who may appear in his behalf shall be declared incompetent to testify.

(21) The witnesses in whose presence instructions are given to the scribe should be personally requested to sign the Get, and should be present when the names of the parties and the date are written in it.

(22) It is necessary that they should know this

to be the Get which the scribe has written in the name of the husband for the wife, and therefore if they desire to leave after it has been written, they should make a mark on it so that they may be able to identify it.

(23) It is advisable that the husband should be present with the scribe and witnesses until it has been written, signed and delivered, that he may not raise any protest against the Get or do anything which might tend to invalidate the proceedings.

(24) If he desires to send the Get to the wife through a messenger, it is necessary that the messenger should be present through the entire proceedings.

(25) It is necessary before the Get is written that he should be informed that he is to be the messenger and the Rabbi should state in his hearing that this Get is written and attested for the woman, in order that the messenger may be afterwards enabled to testify to this fact.

(26) When the Get is sent by a messenger it is advisable that the husband should be solemnly sworn not to raise any protest against the Get or do anything which might invalidate the proceedings and annul the Get.

(27) The husband and the messenger must be of full age, for an infant can neither act as a messenger nor constitute one.

(28) The messenger must be neither a deaf-mute, an idot, an infant, a slave, an idolator, a blind man, or one who has been guilty of a trespass of some Biblical commandment.

(29) The Bill of Divorce should not be delivered by a messenger if the husband and wife are both in the same city.

(30) If the husband is obliged to go away and cannot wait until the Get is written and signed, let him give his directions as above, adding the following: "I hereby constitute........the son of ....a messenger to carry this Get to my wife ....the daughter of........., wherever he may find her, and his hand shall be as my hand and his mouth as my mouth and his act as my act and his delivery as my delivery, and I authorize him to constitute any number of sub-messengers until the Get reaches her hand or the hand of her messenger and as soon as the Get reaches her hand or the hand of her messenger from the hand of .... my messenger or from the hand of any sub-messenger thus constituted, she is divorced from me and is permitted to be married to any man."

(31) He who orders the divorce to be delivered in this manner cannot couple it with conditions.

(32) If he desires that the divorce should not go into effect until after a certain period, he must, when ordering the messenger to deliver the Get to the wife, state that she will not be divorced thereby until after the fixed period of time has expired.

(33) It is not necessary that the messenger should be constituted in the presence of the husband, but he may be constituted by the witnesses (under the direction of the husband) to act as messenger.

NOTE.—This is true only when the husband, for certain reasons, cannot himself hand the Get to the messenger.

(34) Those not competent to act as messengers have been mentioned above.

(35) The messenger must be present during the proceeding, as stated above.

(36) Before the scribe begins to write the Get, he must ask the husband to give him his name and the name of his father and any surnames that they may have.

(37) And it is proper also (where possible) to put the same question to the woman and her father.

(38) The scribe and the witnesses must be to-together during the entire proceeding.

(39) The parchment must be cut to the required size before the writing is commenced.

(40) If the scribe has made a mistake in writing and begins a new Get on the same sheet, he must first cut off the portion of the parchment on which he has written.

(41) The parchment should be greater in length than in breadth.

(42) It should be ruled with thirteen lines, the last line to be divided into two small lines for the signatures of the witnesses, one under the other.

(43) Some say that the writing should be on the side of the parchment which was next to the flesh, and not on the hairy side.

(44) The lines should not be ruled with lead, nor on the same side as the writing.

(45) Some say the Get should not be written with a quill pen.

(46) The writing should be clear and not crooked or confused,

(47) The letters should be separated and not joined together.

(48) Care should be taken not to have the letters of two lines running into each other.

(49) The letters should not extend beyond the marginal line.

(50) There must be no erasures of ink spots; in case ink drops into a letter, a new Get must be written.

(51) If a slip of the pen caused an error, it cannot be erased; a new Get must be written.

(52) There must be no roughness in the letters, and no writing over erasures.

(53) The scribe must be careful to write the form of the Get according to the regulation.

(54) If the Get is found to be improperly written and the husband is still present, he must give the order to write a new one.

(55) When the scribe is about to write he must say to the witnesses: " Behold, I write this Get in the name........the son of........for the purpose of divorcing his wife........the daughter of ...." and then he must proceed to write it at once.

(56) The ink must be dry before the witnesses sign.

(57) And then they sign one under the other.

(58) And in the presence of each other.

(59) Each of the witnesses must state before signing, " I sign this Get in behalf of .... the son of........for the purpose of divorcing with it ....the daughter of........."

(60) The signatures must be placed at the right hand of the sheet next to margin.

(61) Not more than the space of two lines from the last line in the body of the Get.

(62) Each witness must sign his own name and the name of his father, thus, ... the son of .... a witness.

(63) The signatures must be clear and distinct.

(64) The scribe must not be a witness.

(65) The signatures must be dried.

(66) The Rabbi and the witnesses must read the Get together with the signatures of the witnesses, and after they have read it, the Rabbi must ask the scribe, "Is this the Get which you have written at the request of the husband, for the purpose of divorcing his wife .... the daughter of ....?" and he answers "Yes." He then asks one of the witnesses, "Did you hear the husband give the order to the scribe to write the Get?"

(67) "Do you recognize this to be the Get?"

(68) "Did you sign it at the request of the husband?"

(69) "Did you sign it in his behalf and for the purpose of divorcing his wife?"

(70) "Do you recognize your signature?"

(71) "Did you sign it in the presence of the other witness?"

(72) "Do you recognize his signature?"

(73) And the witness answers "Yes" to all of these questions; and in the same manner the second witness is interrogated.

(74) Then the Get is given to the husband and he is asked whether he gives it of his own free will, as above.

(75) The husband then repeats the statement made in paragraph 20.

(76) If the husband leaves before the delivery of the Get, he is sworn not to attempt to invalidate the proceedings, or raise any protest against the Get.

(77) Ten men are summoned to be present at the delivery of the Get.

(78) The Rabbi addresses them, saying: "If any man present knows ought to invalidate the Get or why it should not be delivered, let him speak before it is delivered; for after it is delivered, I shall pronounce the ban of excommunication upon any one who shall attempt to invalidate the Get.

(79) The Rabbi calls upon all competent persons to be witnesses.

(80) It is advisable that the attesting witnesses should be present at the delivery.

(81) The Rabbi shall direct the woman to remove any rings that she may have on her fingers, and stretch forth her hand to receive the Get.

NOTE.—It is customary for the woman to remain veiled until she is thus addressed by the Rabbi. The Rabbi asks her whether she receives the Get of her own free will, and she answers "yes." The Rabbi then inquires about the Kethubah, in order that there may be no dispute regarding it thereafter.

(82) Care must be taken that no one assists her in taking the Get.

(83) She must not close her hand on it until the

husband pronounces the words mentioned in paragraph 84.

(84) The husband places the Get into her hands, saying: "This is thy Get, and thou art divorced by it from me, and art permitted to be married to any man."

(85) After the Get has been laid in her hands, she takes holds of it with both hands, and then the Rabbi takes it from her and reads it for the second time before the witnesses, and pronounces the ban of excommunication on any one who shall attempt to invalidate it.

(86) And then the Rabbi tears the Get crosswise.

(87) He warns the woman not to become betrothed within ninety days from that date.

(88) According to some opinions, the Get should be delivered by day and not by night;

(89) Except in the case of emergency, in which the Get may be written and delivered at night. It must be delivered on the same day on which it was written, except when it is sent to another city and delivery on the same day is impossible.

(90) The husband should not remain alone with his wife between the writing and delivery of the Get, and if he does so, it becomes an "old Get," with which she cannot be divorced.

(91) If the Get is brought to her by a messenger, it must be delivered to her in the presence of two witnesses, and if the messenger is related to her or otherwise incompetent, it is delivered in the presence of at least three, with this statement:

"This is thy Get which thy husband sends thee, and by it thou art divorced from him and free to be married to any man, and this Get was written and signed in my presence."

(92) If the woman is a *Na'arah* (between 12 years and 12 years 6 months of age) she is divorced by personal delivery of the Get to her; if she is betrothed, her father may receive the Get for her, if she has not passed the age of 12 years and 6 months (*Bogereth*).

(93) If she is a *Qetannah* (under the age of 12 years) and has been *married*, her father cannot receive the Get for her.

(94) If she is a *Qetannah* and is *betrothed*, but not yet *married*, her father may receive the Get for her.

(95) A *Qetannah* who does not understand the meaning of a Get cannot be divorced.

(96) When a *Qetannah* is divorced through her father, two Bills of Divorce are written, one in the usual form (for her), and one (intended for her father) reciting the fact that it is for "thy daughter."

(97) If the Get is to be delivered to a messenger to carry it to the wife, he is appointed in the presence of two witnesses, and it is read to him in their presence, and the scribe and the witnesses make their statements before him, as above (paragraphs 66–73).

(98) After this the Rabbi hands the Get to the husband and he hands it to the messenger, saying, "Take this Get to my wife, wherever you may find

her, and your hand shall be as my hand, and your mouth as my mouth, and your act as my act, and your delivery as my delivery, and I authorize you to constitute other messengers and sub-messengers until the Get reaches her hand or the hand of her messenger from your hand, or from the hand of your messenger, or from the hand of the messengers of your messengers, etc.," as above (paragraph 30).

(99) If the divorce is coupled with conditions the husband says to the wife at the time of the delivery: "This is thy Get and thou art hereby divorced from me and free to be married to any man on condition, that if I do not return on this day twelve month thou art divorced from this moment, and if I return within the said period, and appear before........and........this shall not be a Get and I hereby declare that my wife shall be competent to testify that I have not returned and have not been reunited with her."

(100) If the husband is sick he says to her at the time of the delivery: "This is thy Get and thou art divorced by it from me and art free to be married to any man, on condition that if I do not die before (a certain day) this shall not be a Get, but if I die before that time this shall be a Get from this moment."

(101) One should be very careful not to engage in divorce proceedings unless he is learned in the law of divorce, for there are many points to be considered, and it is easy for a man to err therein, and this would result in invalidating the proceeding and in bastardizing children, and may the Rock of Israel save us from all error, Amen.

LIST OF PRINCIPAL WORKS CONSULTED IN THE PREPARATION OF THIS VOLUME.

BIBLE.
MISHNAH.
TALMUD BABLI AND COMMENTARIES.
TALMUD YERUSHALMI.
MEKHILTA.
MIDRASH RABBA.
SEPHER YOKHSIN.
PIRQÉ DI RABBI ELIEZER.
YALKUT SHIMEONI.
ZOHAR.
MOSES BEN MAIMON (Maimonides):
  "Mishné Torah."
SHULHAN ARUKH :
  Eben Haëzer and Commentaries.
  Hoshen Mishpat and Commentaries.
NAHMANIDES' COMMENTARY ON THE PENTATEUCH.
ABEN EZRA'S COMMENTARY ON THE PENTATEUCH.
RASHI'S COMMENTARY ON THE PENTATEUCH.
RESPONSA GAONIM.
PHILO JUDÆUS :
  English Edition of Yonge in Bohn's Library.
JOSEPHUS:
  "Antiquities of the Jews."
  "Life."
INSTITUTES OF GAIUS.
CODE OF JUSTINIAN.

JUSTINIAN'S DIGEST.
NOVELS OF JUSTINIAN.
KORAN:
  English translation, George Sale.
JOSEPH BERGEL:
  " Die Eheverhältnisse der alten Juden im Vergleiche mit den Griechischen und Römischen," Leipzig, 1881.
P. BUCHHOLZ:
  " Die Familie in rechtlicher und moralischer Beziehung nach Mosaisch-Talmudischer Lehre," Breslau, 1867.
CARL HEINRICH CORNILL:
  " Einleitung in das Alte Testament," Freiburg i. B., 1892.
EMANUEL DEUTSCH:
  " The Talmud," Philadelphia, 1895.
M. DUSCHAK:
  " Das Mosaisch-Talmudische Eherecht mit besonderer Rücksicht auf die bürgerlichen Gesetze," Wien, 1864.
H. FASSEL:
  " Das Mosaisch-Rabbinische Civilrecht," Wien, 1852.
Z. FRANKEL:
  " Grundlinien des Mosaisch-Talmudischen Eherechts," Breslau, 1860.
EMIL FRÄNKEL:
  " Das Jüdische Eherecht nach dem Reichs-Civilgesetz vom 6. Februar 1875," München, 1891.
H. GRAETZ:
  " History of the Jews," Philadelphia, 1891.
  " Geschichte der Juden," Leipzig.
IGNAZ GRASZL:
  " Das besondere Eherecht der Juden in Oesterreich," Wien, 1849.
SAMUEL HOLDHEIM:
  " Ueber die Autonomie der Rabbinen und das Princip der Jüdischen Ehe," Schwerin, 1843.
  " Ma'amar Haïshuth," Berlin, 621 (1860).

LIST OF PRINCIPAL WORKS. 207

JULIUS FÜRST:
"Hebräisch-Chaldäisches Handwörterbuch," Leipzig, 1876.

MARCUS JASTROW:
"Dictionary of the Targumim, the Talmud Babli and Yerushalmi, etc."

SAMUEL MAYER:
"Die Rechte der Israeliten, Athener under Römer, etc.," Leipzig, 1861.

JOHANN DAVID MICHAELIS:
"Mosaisches Recht," Biehl, 1777.

M. MIELZINER:
"The Jewish Law of Marriage and Divorce," Cincinnati, 1884.

ISRAEL N. RABBINOWICZ:
"Legislation Civile du Thalmud," Paris, 1880.

J. L. SAALSCHÜTZ:
"Das Mosaische Recht nebst den vervollständigenden Thalmudisch-Rabbinischen Bestimmungen," Berlin, 1853.

MOISE SCHWAB:
"Le Thalmud de Jerusalem."

JOHN SELDEN:
"De Jure naturali et gentium juxta disciplinam Ebræorum," Argentorati, 1665.
"Uxor Ebraica."

EMMANUEL WEILL:
"La femme Juive, sa condition légale d'après la Bible et le Talmud," Paris, 1874.

E. C. WINES:
"Commentaries on the Laws of the Ancient Hebrews," Philadelphia, 1859.

AUGUST WÜNSCHE:
"Der Jerusalemische Talmud in seinen Haggadischen Bestandtheilen," Zürich, 1880.

FUSTEL DE COULANGES:
"The Ancient City," Boston and New York, 1889.

WILLIAM A. HUNTER:
"A Systematic and Historical Exposition of Roman Law," London, 1876.

CHARLES LETOURNEAU:
"The Evolution of Marriage and of the Family," New York (Contemporary Science Series).

FERDINAND MACKELDEY:
"Handbook of the Roman Law," translated and edited by Moses A. Dropsie, Esq., Philadelphia, 1883.

JOHN FERGUSON MCLENNAN:
"Primitive Marriage," London, 1876.

SIR HENRY SUMNER MAINE:
"Ancient Law," New York, 1888.

HERBERT SPENCER:
"The Principles of Sociology," New York, 1886.

W. ROBERTSON SMITH:
"Kinship and Marriage in Early Arabia," Cambridge, 1885.

GLOSSARY.

ABODAH ZARAH. Idolatry; name of a treatise of the Mishnah and Talmud, treating chiefly of the relation between Jews and Heathen, and of Heathen rites and practices; of heresies, etc.

ABOTH. Name of a treatise of the *Mishnah*, containing moral precepts, maxims and apothegms of Talmudic authorities, also styled *Pirqé Aboth*. A similar collection of a later date is contained in *Talmud Babli* editions, named *Aboth d'Rabbi Nathan*.

ABOTH D' RABBI NATHAN. See *Aboth*.

AMORA, pl.: AMORAÏM. That class of Talmudic authorities who lived after the final redaction of the *Mishnah* and whose discussions on the opinions of the *Tannaïm* or authors of the *Mishnah* and *Boraitha* are deposited in the *Gemara*, thus adding a second element to the development of the oral law called *Talmud*.

AMORAÏM. See *Amora*.

BABA BATHRA. See *Baba Qama*.

BABA MEÇIA. See *Baba Qama*.

BABA QAMA. First section (or gate) of three Talmudic treatises, dealing chiefly with the civil law. Baba Qama treats of law of damages and restitution, the other two being called *Baba Meçia*, middle section, treating chiefly of trusts, purchase and sale, and *Baba Bathra*, last section, treating chiefly of laws of real estate and inheritance.

BABLI. *Babylonian*.

BEN. Son of.

BERESHITH RABBAH. Name of the first book of the *Midrash Rabbah*. See *Midrash*.

BETH DIN. Court—literally, House of Justice.

BOGERETH. A female who has passed the age of 12 years and 6 months.

BORAITHA. Traditions and opinions of *Tannaïm* not embodied in the Mishnah as compiled by Rabbi Yehudah.

DEREKH EREÇ. Manners; name of treatise attached to Talmudic editions; containing laws of etiquette and deportment.

EBEL RABBATHI. Great Mourning; name of a Talmudic treatise, also named euphemistically *Semakhoth* (rejoicings), treating of mourning and mourning customs.

EBEN HAËZER. One of the divisions of the *Shulhan Arukh*, treating principally of marriage and divorce.

EDUYOTH. Testimonies; a treatise of the Mishnah and Talmud, containing laws orally transmitted which were proven by distinguished authorities to have been adopted by the Sanhedrin.

EGUNAH. The chained one; the wife who has been deserted by her husband.

ERAKHIN. Valuations; a treatise of the Mishnah and Talmud containing laws relating to consecrated things, vows, etc.

GAON. Excellency; in the post-Talmudic period Gaon was the title of the chiefs of the Babylonian academies.

GEMARA. Memorizing of verbal teachings; tradition; that part of the Talmud containing those discussions, decisions, etc., which after the written compilation of the Mishnah were the materials of verbal study until they, too, were put to writing.

GERUSHIN. Sending off; divorce; name of one of the Treatises of the Code of Maimonides.

GET, pl.: GITTIN. A legal document (used especially in the sense of) a letter of divorce.

GITTIN. Name of a Talmudic treatise; literally, legal documents, especially Bills of Divorce. The Treatise Gittin deals chiefly with the Bill of Divorce and Divorce Procedure.

HALAKHAH. Practice, adopted opinion, rule—hence, law.

HALALAH. The female issue of a priest's illegitimate connection, or of a priest's wife illegitimately married to him.

HALIÇA. The ceremony of taking off the *Yabam's* shoe.

GLOSSARY. 211

HALUÇAH. A woman released from leviratical marriage by Haliça.

HOL HAMMOËD. The half-festive days intervening between the first and the last days of Passover or of Succoth.

HOSHEN HAMISHPAT. The breast-plate of Judgment; one of the divisions of the *Shulḥan Arukh* treating of civil law.

ISHUTH. Matrimony; marital state; name of one of the treatises of the Code of Maimonides.

ISSURÉ BIAH. Name of one of the treatises of the Code of Maimonides.

KETHUBAH, pl.: KETHUBOTH. Writ, deed, especially marriage contract, containing among other things the settlement of a certain amount due to the wife on her husband's death, or on being divorced.

KETHUBOTH. Name of a treatise of Mishnah and Talmud relating to marriage contracts, conjugal rights, etc.

KOHEN, pl.: KOHANIM. Priest; one of the tribe of Aaron.

KUTHI. Cuthean, a member of the sect of the Samaritans.

MAASER SHENI. Second tithe (Deuteronomy xiv, 22, and xxiv, 14) which Levites had to pay to the priests out of their tithes; name of a treatise of the Mishnah.

MAKKOTH. Stripes; name of a treatise of the Mishnah and Talmud containing laws of corporal punishment, of perjury, of involuntary homicide, and of the cities of refuge.

MAMZER. One born of an unlawful, incestuous or adulterous connection.

MEGHILLAH. Scroll; in special sense the Roll of the Book of Esther; a treatise of the Mishnah and Talmud, containing laws relating to the feast of Purim, the reading of the Book of Esther, synagogue public readings of the Scriptures, etc.

MEKHILTA. An ancient commentary to the Book of Exodus.

MELAKHIM. Kings, name of a treatise of the Code of Maimonides.

MIÇVOTH. Commandments.

MIDRASH. The method of discussing the Biblical texts peculiar to the Doctors of the Talmud.

MINA. Coin equal to one hundred shekels.

MISHNAH. A component part of the Talmud; the Code of Law compiled by Rabbi Yehudah the Nasi (about 189 C. E.).

MISHNÉ TORAH. Name of the Code of Moses Maimonides (about 1180).

MISHPATIM. Judgments, name of the sixth section of the Book of Exodus (Cap. xxi, 1—Cap. xxiv, 18).

MOËD QATON. Lesser festival, name of a treatise of the Mishnah and Talmud relating to the middle days of the festivals of Passover and Tabernacles, etc.

NA'ARAH. A female between the ages of 12 years and 12 years 6 months.

NASI. Prince, title of the chief of the Sanhedrin.

NEDARIM. Vows, a treatise of the Mishnah and Talmud relating to vows made by females which the father or husband may annul (Numbers xxx, 4-16).

NETHIN, pl.: NETHINIM. Literally one given or dedicated (to the temple), a descendant of the sacred prostitutes introduced during the reign of the Kings.

PERUTAH. The smallest copper coin known to the Jews.

PESSAHIM. Name of a treatise of the Mishnah and Talmud relating to the Passover, sacrifice of Paschal lamb, etc.

PIRQÉ ABOTH. See *Aboth*.

PIRQÉ D'RABBI ELIEZER. An Haggadistic work on the Pentateuch of about the eighth century, falsely ascribed to Rabbi Eliezer ben Hyrcanus.

QETANNAH. A female under the age of 12 years.

QIDDUSHIN. Name of a treatise of the Mishnah and Talmud relating to betrothals.

RABBAN. (Teacher), the title of the chief of the Sanhedrin.

RABBI. My master, title of a Doctor of the Law.

SANHEDRIN. Name of a treatise of the Mishnah and Talmud relating to the constitution of the Courts of Law, etc.

SEDER HA-GET. Rules of Procedure in giving a Bill of Divorce.

SEPHER YOKHSIN. Book of Genealogies of Talmudic authorities.

SHABBATH. Sabbath, name of a treatise of the Mishnah and Talmud relating to observance of Sabbath day.

GLOSSARY. 213

SHEBUOTH. Oaths, name of a treatise of the Mishnah and Talmud relating to administration of oaths.
SHULHAN ARUKH. The Prepared Table, name of the Code of Rabbi Joseph Karo (about 1554).
SOTAH. Name of a treatise of the Mishnah and Talmud containing laws relating to the woman suspected of adultery (Numbers v. 11–31).
TALMUD. A method of legal reasoning peculiar to the Rabbis; a name for the Mishnah and Gemara, considered as a whole.
TANNA, pl.: TANNAÏM. Learner, or repeater, the title of the Doctors of the Law during the period of the Mishnah (about 220 B. C. E.–220 C. E.).
TANNAÏM. See *Tanna*.
TEBUL YOM. Name of a treatise of the Mishnah relating to the laws of purification by ablutions on the day the uncleanness has been contracted.
THERUMOTH. Heave offerings, name of a treatise of the Mishnah.
TORAH. Legal precept, especially the Law, *i. e.*, Pentateuch as distinguished from the other portions of the Bible.
TURIM. Name of the Code compiled by Rabbi Jacob ben Asher (about 1340).
YABAM. Brother-in-law, who in the case of his brother dying without issue, enters his estate and marries his wife (Deuteronomy xxv, 5, etc.).
YADAYIM. Hands, name of a treatise of the Mishnah, containing laws for purifying the hands from uncleanness.
YEBAMA. Sister-in-law, the widow of a brother who died without issue.
YEBAMOTH. The legal relations between *Yabam* and *Yebama*, name of a treatise of the Mishnah and Talmud.
YERUSHALMI. Of Jerusalem; *Talmud Yerushalmi*, the Palestinean collection of Mishnah and Gemara in con tradistinction to the Babli (Babylonian collection).
ZOHAR. Shining; name of a Kabbalistic work of the thirteenth century.
ZUZ. A silver coin, one-fourth of a shekel—denar.

INDEX.

	PAGE
Abba Areka,	69, 173 n.
Abba Saul,	124
Abraham, divorces Hagar,	23, 133
Adulteress, must leave her husband,	42
loses her Kethubah,	122
cannot marry paramour,	96
Adultery,	42, 83, 86, 93, 96, 107
Agent, see *Messenger*.	
of husband could not delegate powers,	151
doctrine of agency founded on Biblical law,	177
Aha, Rabbi,	135, 191
Amemar,	125
Ami, Rabbi,	65, 76
Amoraim,	17
Annulment of the Get,	48, 87, 186, 187
Antenuptial Incontinence,	28, 41, 47, 63, 122
Apostasy, does not destroy marriage relation,	75
Aqiba, Rabbi,	33, 37, 85, 116, 152
Arabian form of divorce,	136
Assi, Rabbi,	129
Attestation of the Get,	171
Augustus,	139
Aversion, unconquerable, reason for divorce,	125
Babylonia, centre of Jewish life,	18
Bald Get	159
Bar Kokhba, divorce regulations after the rebellion of,	119, 140, 132 n., 183
Barrators excommunicated,	187
Barrenness, cause of divorce,	87, 99, 124
Bedouin, divorce among the,	137
Betrothed, divorce of,	77

INDEX.

	PAGE
Bigamy, cause of divorce,	99
Bill of Divorce,	
views of Sadducees on,	16
peculiar to the Jews,	59, 135
soldier's,	134, 170
ordering,	143
writing,	148
attesting,	171
delivering,	174
oldest form of,	132
form of,	156
essential parts of,	161
torn crosswise on payment of Kethubah,	118
when void, consequences,	49
effect of,	105
"Old Get,"	81
"Folded Get,"	159
"Bald Get,"	159
when lost,	81, 188
Bitter waters, ordeal of the,	93
Blank forms of Get, use of,	158
Bondswoman, rights of,	55
Captive, wife taken	46
Causes for divorce,	
adultery,	83
antenuptial incontinence,	42
apostasy,	75
aversion,	125
barrenness,	99
bigamy,	76
desertion,	73
expatriation,	126
immorality,	123
impotence,	65
leprosy,	67
licentiousness,	76
mutual consent,	39
physical blemishes,	67

INDEX. 217

	PAGE
refusal of conjugal rights,	63
refusal to support,	68
sterility,	99
wife-beating,	70
divorce rarely without cause,	104
dispute of schools of Hillel and Shammai about	32
Childlessness	65, 99
Children, legitimacy of,	85
of divorced woman	127
custody of,	129
support of,	130
Christian, marriage of Jew and,	92
Codes, Jewish law,	12, 17, 18, 19
Condition, divorce on,	165
Condonation of adultery not allowed,	96
Confession of adultery, effect of,	96
Conflict of Jewish and non-Jewish law,	141
Conjugal rights a cause for divorce, refusal of,	63, 124
Consanguinity,	124
Construction of language of Get,	145
Contractual character of marriage,	56
Court will force husband to give divorce,	58, 89
of the Jews in criminal cases,	178
of Gentiles, appeal to,	75
divorce in court of heathen,	59, 135, 149
Custody of children,	127, 129
Damages to be paid by ravisher and seducer,	43, 44
Dating the Get,	16, 161
Day, legal,	164
Deaf-Mute cannot divorce,	50, 51, 148
cannot be messenger for divorce,	179
Death from absence, no presumption of,	72, 169
statement made, or act done in contemplation of,	146
penalty,	84
divorce on condition of husband's,	169
Delivery of Get to the wife,	174, etc.
Desertion,	72, 75, 126

14

218   INDEX.

	PAGE
Dies juridici,	163
Diffareatio,	139
Diocletian, laws of,	129, 140
Divorce, reference in Bible to,	12, 23, 30
a necessary evil,	25, 37
is pre-Mosaic,	25, 132
is a quasi-religious act,	59, 141, 179
is a quasi-judicial act,	143
by the Court,	58, 89
rarely without cause,	1c4
by mutual consent,	39
begins at delivery of Get,	175
among Arabs,	136
Greeks,	138
Romans,	61, 138
Bedouin,	137
heathen,	135
on condition,	165, etc.
proof of,	188
Divorced woman may remarry,	84, 98
is *sui juris*,	101, 105
entitled to custody of children,	129
remarriage of,	107
maintenance of,	121
property of,	111
vow of,	106, 108, 128
Dowry, see Kethubah,	46, 111
Duress, invalidates divorce,	57
Earnings, etc., of divorced woman,	121
Egunah,	73, 146, 181
Elazar, Rabbi,	38, 87
Eliezer, Rabbi,	158, 165, 172
Eliezer ben Parta, Rabbi,	178
Equitable rules become law,	79
Ervath Dabar,	33
Essential parts of a Get,	161
words of separation,	164
Expatriation,	126

INDEX. 219

	PAGE
Ezra's ordinance,	90
Fees of scribe for writing Get,	153
Fine, paid by seducer and ravisher,	43
Folded Get,	159
Foreign parts, Get sent from,	180, etc.
Gamaliel, Rabban,	171
Gamaliel the Elder, Rabban,	48, 49, 164, 186
Gershom of Mayence, decree of Rabbi,	24, 52, 76
Get, see Bill of Divorce.	
Greeks, form of divorce among the,	138
Hadrian, decree of, respecting Jewish divorces,	119, 140, 152 n., 183
Hagar, divorce of,	23, 127
Haliça,	98, 144, 177
Hallalah,	98
Hanina, Rabbi,	151, 173 n.
Hasda, Rabbi,	129, 130, 173 n.
Heathen, marriage with,	89
may not be messenger,	179
divorce in Court of the,	59, 135, 149
Herodias divorced her husband,	61
Hillel,	37, 64, 81, 128
schools of Shammai and,	32
Hosha'yah, Rabbi,	121
Huna, Rabbi,	135
Husband has right to divorce wife,	24
right to divorce restricted,	41
is compelled to divorce at suit of wife,	58
insane, cannot divorce	50
must support children	128
must himself order the Get,	147
may attach conditions to Get,	165
cannot condone adultery of wife,	42, 196
annulment of bill of divorce, (see annulment),	48
Impotence, cause for divorce,	65
Incest,	89
Insanity of husband,	50
of wife,	45

	PAGE
Isaiah,	134
Ishmael, Rabbi,	45, 173
Isserles, Rabbi Moses	71
Jacob bar Aḥa, Rabbi	110
Jephthah's sacrifice,	23
Jeremiah,	82, 160
Jerusalem, residence in,	73, 127
Jesus' opinions on divorce,	26, 35, 61, 84
Joseph, Rabbi,	178
Joseph and Mary, case of,	35
Josephus' opinions on divorce,	34, 61
Joshua, Rabbi,	88
Joshua ben Qorḥa, Rabbi,	177
Judicial separation,	89
divorce is quasi,	143
Justinian,	130
Kahana, Rabbi,	70
Kethubah, laws relating to,	111-127
purpose of,	47, 48
guarantee of,	87
King, divorced wife of,	138
Kohen, see priest.	
Legitimacy of children,	85
Leprosy, cause for divorce,	67, 97
Levirate marriage,	144, 147, 169
Liberty of wife, personal,	69
Licentiousness, cause for divorce,	75
Lost Get,	81, 188
Maimonides,	14, 18, 53, 156
Maine, Sir H. S.	9, 10
Maintenance of children,	130
Majority, rule of,	20
Malachi's protest against divorce,	30
Mamzer.	93
Maintenance, see support.	
Manumission of slave, bill of,	149, 186
Mar Raba,	125
Marriage, Jewish view of,	39

INDEX. 221

	PAGE
Marriage with divorced woman,	84
to second wife,	82
of divorced woman,	107
of deaf-mute,	51
form of,	137
of adulteress to paramour prohibited,	96
clauses in Get in restraint of,	164, 167
Mar Samuel,	69, 99, 129, 137, 140
Meïr, Rabbi,	38, 86, 114
Messenger in divorce proceedings, laws relating to,	107, 177–185
Military divorces,	134, 170
Minor wife,	46, 124, 189
Mishnah,	13, 15, 16, 17, 45
Mohammed,	64, 84, 109, 115, 137
Mohammedan law,	71, 84, 141
Montaigne on divorce,	37
Morality, breach of, ground for divorce,	123
Mosaic law,	11–15, 17, 23, 25, 28–30, 41, 43–47, 55, 63, 66, 79, 82, 89, 93, 109, 122, 127, 132
Mute, divorce by a,	148
Mutual Consent, divorce by,	39
Names of parties in Get,	164
Nehemiah,	92
Nethin,	93, etc.
Nurslings remain with divorced wife	128
Obadiah of Bartenora, Rabbi,	159
Old Get,	81
Ordeal of bitter waters	93, etc.
Ordering the Get	143
Palestine, residence in,	73, 126
Paramour could not marry adulteress,	96
Patriarchal system,	22, 54, 101, 127, 149, 165
Paul, on divorce, opinion of,	36, 84
Pharisees, views on the law	16
views on divorce,	162
Jesus and the,	35
Philo,	34, 83, 99, 102

Physical blemishes cause for divorce, ... 44, 67, 122
Polygamy abolished, ... 53, 76
Practice and theory of divorce, ... 32
Preparing the Get, ... 143
Presumption of remarriage, ... 81
   of death, ... 146
   of life, ... 177
Priest, could not marry a captive, ... 34, n. 3
   must divorce wife if unclean, ... 66
   could not marry divorced woman, ... 98, 109
   could not marry harlot or Ḥallalah, ... 102
   high priest could not marry a widow, ... 103
   law of priest's daughter, ... 104
   could not remarry his own divorced wife, . . 160
   rights of priest's wife, ... 182
Procedure in divorce, rules of, ... 142, 192, etc.
Proof of divorce, ... 188
Property of divorced woman, ... 111
Rab, ... 69, 173 n.
Raba Mar, ... 125
Raba bar Rab Huna, ... 173, etc.
Rabbinical law, authority of, ... 13, 20
Rabbinowicz, J. M., ... 160
Rabha 38
Rape, see Ravisher.
Rashi, ... 159
Ravisher, ... 29, 42 114
Reconciliation, ... 47, 79
Refusal of conjugal rights, cause for divorce, . . . 117, 124
Religious act, divorce a quasi- 59, 141, 179
   uses, ... 87
   obstructions, ... 44
Remarriage of divorced woman, ... 30, 81, 82, 109
Renunciation of right to remarry, ... 87
Restraint of marriage clauses in Get, in 164, 167
Restrictions on divorce, 24, 26, 28, 41, 45, 46, 48, 50, 69, 76, 107
Roman law, father's power, ... 23
   divorce, ... 61
   loss of citizenship, ... 75

INDEX.   223

	PAGE
presumption of death,	73
introduction of bill of divorce,	139
form of divorce,	138
Rules of procedure in divorce,	192
Rumor, effect of,	190
Sadducees,	16, 162
Salome divorced her husband,	61
Samuel bar Abba, Mar,	69, 99, 129, 137, 140
Samuel bar Naḥmani,	170
Sanhedrin, of Mayence,	52
of Troyes,	187
Saul, king, exercises patria-potestas	23
Schools of law,	18
Sealed Get,	160
Seder Ha-Get,	192, etc.
Seduction,	29 n., 43
Separate estate of wife,	120
Separation, words of,	164
Sexual immorality, cause for divorce,	33
Shammai,	64, 81, 128
Schools of Hillel and	32
Shimeon ben Shetaḥ,	113
Shulḥan Arukh,	19, 53
Simon ben Gamaliel, Rabban, 67, 70, 87, 108, 119, 145, 160	
Simon III ben Gamaliel, Rabban,	49
Simon ben Shetaḥ,	113
Simon ben Yoḥai,	150
Simon the Just,	14, 15
Slander,	28
Slave,	149, 179
Spencer, Herbert, on divorce,	40 n.
Status of divorced woman,	101
Sterility, cause for divorce	99
Stripes, punishment by,	39, 89, 109
Support, wife entitled to,	55
refusal to,	67
of divorced woman,	121
of children,	130
Talmud,	10, 12, 18

	PAGE
Tannaim,	16
Tarphon, Rabbi,	124
Torah, see Mosaic law.	
Torts, liability of divorced woman for,	106
Traditional law,	12, 13, 14
Turim,	19
Ulla, Rabbi,	129, 131
Vow of wife, annulment of,	66, 69, 70
of abstention,	66
to divorce,	79
absolving from,	80
of divorced woman,	106, 108, 128
Waiver of Kethubah,	114
Weil, Rabbi Jacob,	71
Wife, falsely accused of antenuptial incontinence,	41
right to a divorce,	54, 57
personal rights under Biblical law,	24, 55, 55 n.
cannot be divorced against her will,	52
cannot give Get to her husband,	60
beating,	70, 71
must have a Kethubah,	114
pays scribe's fees,	154
may appoint messenger,	182
could write her own Get,	149
Witnesses, subscribing to Get,	172
must know the parties,	172
at delivery of Get,	174
divorced woman her own witness,	188
Writing, the Get,	148, etc.
order to write,	144, 147
Yannai, Rabbi,	20, 45
Yebama,	98, 145
Yehudah, the Nasi, Rabbi, 15, 17, 117, 124, 158, 164, 169, 183	
Yehudah ben Bathyra, Rabbi,	154
Yohanan, Rabbi,	38, 135, 189
Yohanan ben Zakkai, Rabbi,	97
Yosé, Rabbi,	124, 152, 169
Yosé ben Yehudah, Rabbi,	114
Yosé, the Galilean, Rabbi,	110, 154

www.ingramcontent.com/pod-product-compliance
Lightning Source LLC
Chambersburg PA
CBHW021830230426
43669CB00008B/919